CHRISTIAN HEROES: THEN & NOW

BETTY GREENE

Wings to Serve

CHRISTIAN HEROES: THEN & NOW

BETTY GREENE

Wings to Serve

JANET & GEOFF BENGE

P.O. BOX 55787   SEATTLE, WA 98155

YWAM Publishing is the publishing ministry of Youth With A Mission. Youth With A Mission (YWAM) is an international missionary organization of Christians from many denominations dedicated to presenting Jesus Christ to this generation. To this end, YWAM has focused its efforts in three main areas: (1) training and equipping believers for their part in fulfilling the Great Commission (Matthew 28:19), (2) personal evangelism, and (3) mercy ministry (medical and relief work).

For a free catalog of books and materials, call (425) 771-1153 or (800) 922-2143. Visit us online at www.ywampublishing.com.)

Betty Greene: Wings to Serve

13 12 11 10 09   4 5 6 7 8 9

Published by Youth With A Mission Publishing
P.O. Box 55787
Seattle, WA 98155

ISBN 13: 978-1-57658-152-0
ISBN 10: 1-57658-152-7

Printed in the United States of America.

CHRISTIAN HEROES: THEN & NOW

*Unit study curriculum guides
are available for select biographies.*

*Available at your local Christian
bookstore or from YWAM Publishing
1-800-922-2143 / www.ywampublishing.com*

Acknowledgments

Special thanks to Dietrich Buss for making available to us a copy of the as yet unpublished autobiographical manuscript titled *Flying High: The Story of Betty Greene*. Mr. Buss helped Betty Greene prepare this informative manuscript shortly before her death, and his help proved an invaluable source in writing this book.

Thanks also to Al and Bill Greene for their patience in answering so many questions about their sister.

Countries in which Betty Greene Served

Irian Jaya
Sudan
Nigeria
Mexico
Peru

Contents

Chapter 1

Target Practice

The twin-engine Lockheed B-34 bomber stood illuminated in pools of white floodlight on a corner of the tarmac. Betty Greene strolled toward it, her parachute strapped securely to her back and her fur-lined flying jacket buttoned tight against the crisp fall air. Her heart beat wildly as she approached the airplane. She climbed into the cockpit and pulled the safety belt snug around her. Already sitting in the copilot's seat beside her was the officer in charge. This was Betty's first flight in a Lockheed B-34, and he was going along to check Betty out in the aircraft.

"I'll watch while you put her through the motions," grunted the officer in a disinterested, almost disrespectful way.

Betty methodically began working through her preflight procedures. She checked the fuel level in each of the plane's tanks. "Tank one full. Tank two at the three-quarter mark," she called. Next she adjusted her seat, moving it to the farthest back position. Someone much shorter than she had obviously flown the plane last. Next she pulled her earphones on and checked the radio switches.

With the first stage of preparations over, she turned her attention to the cockpit controls. As she adjusted the rudder, unlocked the controls, and made sure the parking brake was on, the officer beside her said, "You seem to know what you're doing. Any questions?"

"No, sir," Betty replied. "So far, so good."

"Well, in that case, wake me if you need me," the officer replied.

Betty glanced over at the officer, thinking he was joking. But to her surprise—and her dismay—he had slid his seat back as far as it would go and had already settled down for a nap.

Despite the officer's lax attitude, Betty continued with her preflight check. Looking out the cockpit window, she made sure the flaps were working, and then she set them for takeoff. Next she checked the throttle control and primed the engines. "Clear," she called twice, leaning out the cockpit window, and then flicked a switch to start the engines. First one and then the other burst to life.

Once the engines were both purring smoothly, Betty released the brake and pushed the throttle forward to rev the engines. The B-34 rolled forward. Betty talked to the control tower on the radio as she started to taxi the plane across the tarmac. A controller instructed her to proceed to the end of the runway and hold position. Once she had brought the airplane to a halt, three men hauling a cable scurried to the back of the plane, where they attached the cable to a metal eyelet at the back of the tail. As the men scurried back, one of them ran to the front, where Betty could see him from the cockpit, and gave her a thumbs-up. Betty radioed the control tower for permission to take off. Soon the Lockheed was barreling down the runway before lifting into the cool, dark, moonless night. The cable at the back of the plane was taut as it dragged a large canvas square with an enormous bull's-eye painted on it behind the plane.

"Head to two thousand feet," mumbled the officer, without opening his eyes.

Betty adjusted the flaps, keeping the throttle on full. She eased the joystick forward a little and then banked to the left in a wide circle as she gained altitude. There was little to see below except the lights in the distance of one or possibly two small boats bobbing about in the Atlantic Ocean. Once she reached two thousand feet, Betty leveled off the plane and proceeded to make a pass over the range where the antiaircraft gunners were practicing.

All at once, an enormous burst of light exploded about twenty yards off the right side of the aircraft. Betty's eyes widened as she realized how close the live shells from the antiaircraft guns were to the plane. She glanced over at the commanding officer, who was curled up and snoring in his seat. Betty's mind raced. It was her first time pulling targets for gunnery practice. Was this normal? Should she wake the officer and ask him whether shells ought to be exploding so close to the airplane? The officer, like most of the men stationed at Camp Davis, North Carolina, was not very enthusiastic about having women pilots serving there, and Betty worried that he might reprimand her for being a nervous woman if she woke him.

Another burst of gunfire exploded beside them. This time it was close enough to light up the entire cockpit with an eerie glow. Betty decided that no matter what the commanding officer said, she was going to wake him. Just then, another burst of gunfire whizzed past the plane. As it did so, the officer sat bolt upright. "What was that?" he yelled.

"Shells are exploding all around us. Is that normal?" Betty asked.

"Normal, normal!" the officer spluttered. "Some fool down there is aiming right at us and not the target! What are they trying to do, shoot us down?"

Frantically the officer reached for the radio. He barked some orders into the microphone, and within two minutes, the shells had stopped exploding around the Lockheed B-34. Betty breathed a sigh of relief and noticed the officer seemed to have suddenly lost interest in sleeping.

Betty made several more passes over the antiaircraft gunnery range. This time the gunner's sights were aimed on the target being towed behind and not on the B-34 itself. As she flew, Betty marveled at how she was fulfilling her childhood dream to one day fly. She was a member of the Women Airforce Service Pilots. She flew military aircraft in logistical and support roles, and her accomplishments in the air were helping America's war effort. Yet she also had a higher purpose for her flying. Being a part of the Women Airforce Service Pilots was just a stepping-stone on the path to achieving her real goal: combining her love of God with her love of flying to serve others. But that night it all seemed to her a long way from the life she had known growing up in Seattle on the shores of Lake Washington.

Chapter 2

A Great Aviator

Eight-year-old Betty Greene pushed a strand of long brown hair out of her eyes and peered upward for a glimpse of the *Spirit of St. Louis*. She had read everything she could about Charles Lindbergh and his amazing flight from Long Island, New York, to Paris. She had to pinch herself to remind herself she really was in the stadium at the University of Washington waiting with thousands of other excited people for her hero to fly overhead.

Betty wiggled a little closer to her oldest brother, Joe. Even though Joe was sixteen years old, Betty felt they were buddies. After all, the two of them shared a love for airplanes. Joe already had a pilot's license, having flown solo at fourteen, and Betty could hardly wait to follow in his footsteps.

An eerie hush fell over the crowd. Then Betty heard it: the buzz of an airplane engine in the distance. The sound grew steadily louder. Betty squinted into the sun until she finally saw the plane come into view. The tiny single-engine monoplane glistened in the sunlight. On each side of its nose, the words *Spirit of St. Louis* were painted in blue script lettering, and the call letters N-X-211 were emblazoned on the underside of the right wing. Betty gazed in amazement as the plane circled the stadium three times. Her imagination ran wild. She was actually looking at the first airplane ever to fly nonstop across the Atlantic Ocean. She had followed the attempts of other pilots to be the first to make the 3,600-mile nonstop flight. Commander David had crashed his plane in a trial flight, killing himself and his copilot. Captain Nuingesser, a French pilot, had taken off from Paris in a biplane and was never seen again. But now, right overhead, were the airplane and the pilot who had made the thirty-three-and-one-half-hour flight on May 22, 1927. After a final tip of its wings, the airplane climbed and headed southwest.

"Where's it going?" Betty asked Joe.

"To Sand Point Naval Air Station," he replied. "Lindbergh is going to land there, and then a motorcade will bring him back to the stadium. See that stand down there?" He pointed to a large wooden platform decorated with red, white, and blue ribbons. "That's where he will give a speech and receive his medal from the City of Seattle."

Betty turned to her twin brother Bill and relayed the thrilling news to him. Bill nodded, though Betty was sure he would be thinking more about the car Lindbergh arrived in than the airplane he'd flown across the Atlantic. Despite being born only eight minutes apart, Bill did not share Betty's interest in airplanes, though they enjoyed and did almost everything else together. They gathered wild blackberries from the bushes at the edge of Lake Washington, which formed the western boundary of the Greene family's property. They were in the same class at Hunts Point School. And being the youngest, they were both fed and bathed by Josephine, the family maid, who tucked them safely into bed each night before their father arrived home from the office at 6 P.M. One thing the Greene twins did not lack was plenty of fresh air, sunshine, and sleep.

At last Betty heard the honking of horns. All those around her rose to their feet, chanting "Lindbergh, Lindbergh" and waving souvenir flags with the famous aviator's face on them. Some people wore hats with shiny commemorative buttons on them or carried tiny dolls dressed in pilot's leathers.

Betty stood on her tiptoes. Squeezed between Joe and her other brother, twelve-year-old Albert, she tried to peer through the sea of hats that blocked her view. She couldn't see a thing. Finally she looked up at Joe with tears stinging her brown eyes. With an understanding look, Joe scooped her up and held her above the crowd so that she could see.

Suddenly there he was! The greatest aviator of the time—Charles Lindbergh—had arrived. He looked like an overgrown, gangly schoolboy. Betty was surprised, as she had expected someone who looked older and wiser, like her father. "Lucky" Lindbergh, as he had been nicknamed, sat in the backseat of a big open car, grinning from ear to ear. As he drove past, no more than fifteen feet from her, Betty could make out the Distinguished Flying Cross pinned to the left side of his jacket that President Coolidge had presented to him.

The cheering and applause of the crowd finally died down, and the speeches began. Betty couldn't follow all that was said; it was a blur of information about the Ryan plane Lindbergh had flown, how safe it was, and how flying was the future for America. Charles Lindbergh also said something about America having an airport in every city and town someday. It all sounded far-fetched to Betty, but she hoped it was true. There was nothing she wanted to do more than fly.

In the following years, other, more important concerns occupied Betty's mind. In May of 1928, the Greene family suffered through a disaster. The twins, Betty and Bill, were at a birthday party for one of their second-grade classmates. As Betty's mother, Gertrude Greene, was helping to serve the cake, the telephone rang. Mrs. Greene answered it, and Betty watched as her mother's face fell. She knew something was wrong. "Yes, yes, thank you. I understand," she heard her mother say just before she put the phone down and ran outside. The entire birthday party followed her. They all rushed to the side of the road, where about a quarter of a mile away they could see flames shooting high into the air.

"A fire," yelled one of the children in delight.

Betty did not share the boy's excitement. Her stomach was tied in knots. It was her house that was engulfed in flames.

Later that night, when the embers had cooled, the Greene family inspected what had once been their spacious home, now a pile of blackened wood. Grotesque twisted skeletons of their furniture lay scattered among the ruins. Betty could make out the bedsprings where her bed had been and a broken piece of her favorite doll china tea set. Nothing was left except two lawn chairs that had been on the back porch. Someone had dashed up and rescued them. Evergreen Point's only firefighting equipment, a hose pushcart, had been no match for the fire that engulfed the tinder-dry solid cedar home.

Thankfully a small cottage was on the property, and the Greene family crammed into it for the time being. Friends and neighbors brought clothes and kitchen items, and before long, life felt almost normal again. However, an even bigger disaster was brewing across America. October 29, 1929, "Black Tuesday," as it came to be known, was a tragic day for many people, who on that day discovered that the stocks and bonds they'd invested in had lost their value. The Wall Street crash had begun. Financial panic gripped the nation. The wheels of industry ground to a halt as the price of everything from produce to machinery collapsed. Unemployment spread throughout the country as rapidly as fire had through the Greenes' home.

America was in shock. Most people had thought the good years following World War I would go on forever. Now they were suddenly plunged into what became known as the Great Depression.

Betty Greene was nine years old at the time, and although she didn't understand much about stocks and bonds, she knew for certain that some things had changed. Her father now came home from work with a worried look on his face. Albert Greene owned a small business called Greene Electric Furnace Company. He had developed a special design for making arc furnaces for steel mills, which he sold to the biggest steel manufacturers in the country. When the economy collapsed, people stopped buying new cars and other items made of steel. This meant that there was no demand for steel, and so the manufacturers had no reason to buy Mr. Greene's new furnaces for their mills.

The Great Depression also meant that Josephine, the family maid, had to be dismissed. In her place, Betty's mother did all the housework herself. As well, the new seven-passenger V-8 Lincoln touring car Mr. Greene had just purchased was put up on wooden blocks in the garage. The family could no longer afford to buy gasoline for it.

Both Betty and Bill got summer jobs to help their mother pay for groceries. One summer they picked cherries for several weeks. The pay wasn't great—just seventy-five cents a week—but they got to eat as many cherries as they could, and then some! Betty, who loved animals, found a small black-and-white dog in the cherry orchard. The dog attached itself to her, and soon Betty had a new friend, which she named Shep.

Mr. Greene had been wise with his money, and the Greene family were better off than many others. Betty and Bill continued to go to school, and even though their clothes were no longer new, they always looked well cared for.

In sixth grade, the twins had a teacher from Germany. The teacher loved to read to the class, especially books about air warfare during World War I, and how German and English pilots in their flimsy biplanes had engaged in dogfights. Betty loved to listen to these stories, not so much the bits about the shooting and bombings, but about the planes soaring high in the air, looping and doing daring acrobatics. As she sat listening to the teacher read, she had no idea that one day she would be a pilot in another war.

Shep, the stray dog, followed Betty and Bill everywhere, and it made Betty yearn for more pets. In particular she had her sights set on a horse. The family's two-acre property, which sloped down to Lake Washington, had plenty of room for a horse, but was there enough money for one? Eventually, Betty won out, and her parents agreed to buy her a horse if she promised to take good care of it. Dixie cost eight dollars, and Betty faithfully shoveled out the barn and spread hay for her every day. She also loved to ride Dixie, especially since her mother allowed her to wear jodhpurs instead of the skirts and dresses she had to wear the rest of the time. Betty would gallop Dixie down the dusty back roads, stopping along the way to talk to friends from the Sunday school her parents oversaw. She also loaned Dixie to Bill so that he could deliver the *Saturday Evening Post* to about fifty families on a five-mile route around the neighborhood.

When she wasn't riding, Betty spent her time reading or going to the movies. So many interesting things were happening in the world. In 1928 Amelia Earhart had become the first woman to fly across the Atlantic Ocean (as a passenger, but it was still considered a daring feat), and she had followed that up with several adventurous solo flights in the United States. In 1929 Richard Byrd and Bernt Balchen had become the first two people to fly to the South Pole.

Of course, reading about all these aviators' accomplishments just made Betty yearn to fly even more. On her sixteenth birthday, Betty finally got her wish. Her father arranged for her and Bill to take an airplane ride. Flying was all Betty had imagined it would be—and more. She was hooked! That same birthday her uncle gave the twins one hundred dollars each. That was a lot of money, and the two of them agonized over what to do with it. Bill eventually decided to save his for college, but Betty knew she wanted to take flying lessons more than anything else. Her parents agreed to let her use most of the money for that purpose, as long as she used a portion of it to buy herself some new clothes.

Within days, Betty was bumping down the runway with her instructor, Elliot Merrill, at the controls. She watched everything he did, from the way he worked the rudder with his feet to how he set the flaps for takeoff and landing.

Two weeks later, Betty was flying solo and enjoying every moment of it, although she never got as far as earning her private pilot's license before her money ran out.

Now that they were sixteen years old, school was coming to an end for the Greene twins. It was time for them to make some serious career choices. Bill had always planned to attend California Institute of Technology to earn an engineering degree as his father had, but even with a partial scholarship, there simply wasn't enough money in the family budget. Instead Bill settled for studying mining engineering at the nearby University of Washington. Betty, who had hoped to attend a women's college, was also forced to choose the University of Washington, which she could attend while still living at home.

The question was, what should she study? Mrs. Greene had very definite ideas about what her daughter should pursue. She believed nursing was a suitable career for a young woman. It was useful and socially acceptable. Betty wasn't so convinced. She loved animals and airplanes and dreamed of having a career involving either or both of these. But what kind of job? Eventually Betty gave in and let her mother have her way. She entered the University of Washington to study for a bachelor's degree in science with a nursing major. It was the winter of 1937, and it looked to seventeen-year-old Betty as if a predictable future had been neatly laid out for her. Little did she know what adventures lay just around the corner!

Chapter 3

Avenger Field

It was winter 1937, and life had fallen into a pattern for the Greene twins, Betty and Bill. In the morning they would eat breakfast with their parents and then pack their satchels for a day at the university. As Betty made her bed, she would keep an ear open for the sound of the steam whistle. "Come on, Bill," she would yell when she heard it. The two of them would grab their bags and head for the door. Outside they would race each other to the dock. Usually it was a tie. Betty was very fit, and at five feet, ten inches tall, she had the build of a professional runner. But Bill, who was three inches taller, was a good match for her. When they got to the dock, they would stand panting while they waited for the passenger ferry to dock so they could climb aboard for the two-mile trip to the western shore of Lake Washington. From the dock on the other side of the lake, it was a five-mile walk to the University of Washington campus.

Betty loved traveling on the old steam ferry. The ride, along with the walk to and from the university, was the highlight of her day. The time she actually spent in class was not at all exciting. Her courses were a blur of studying anatomy and physiology, dissecting cadavers (dead bodies), and learning about infectious diseases. Betty tried her best to find something about her nursing training that she liked. It was no use; the truth was, she hated the training. And things only got worse. In her second year, she started training at Harborview Hospital in Seattle. Life became a round of changing bandages, checking patients' vital signs, emptying bedpans, and making an endless number of beds, each with the hospital stripe on the blanket stretched perfectly straight down the center. As the days dragged on, Betty knew she had to find some way to get out of her predicament.

Betty pleaded with her mother to be allowed to drop out of the course, but dropping out was not in the Greene family's vocabulary. Still, Mrs. Greene must have seen how unhappy her daughter was, because she discussed the situation with her husband. Together they decided that Betty should stick to her nursing training for one more quarter. If at the end of that time she still did not like nursing, she would be allowed to drop out of the course. Betty accepted her parents' conditions, and to her great relief, she withdrew from the nursing program in the spring of 1939.

Although she had left nursing, Betty had no idea what she was going to do next. All she knew was that something was missing in her life. She needed some sense of adventure, some reason for which to jump out of bed each morning.

While she searched for this adventure, Betty helped her father in his office and assisted with the youth group at the First Presbyterian Church of Seattle, which she attended each Sunday. She also listened to the radio and read the newspaper every morning. The Great Depression had finally ended, but it was being replaced with something worse: war. In September 1939, Germany invaded Poland, and when the German government refused requests to withdraw its troops, England and France declared war. The United States had not officially taken sides in the war, but in October 1940, men were conscripted into the armed forces in the first peacetime call-up for compulsory military service in the history of the country.

In 1940 Betty also said farewell to her older brother Albert and his wife, Thelma, who were headed to China as missionaries. It was a tense time to be traveling anywhere in the world. From a safety standpoint, China was a particularly bad choice of places to go. It had been at war with Japan for several years, and two weeks after Al and Thelma Greene arrived in Shanghai, all foreigners were ordered to leave. The two of them were determined to stay and help the Chinese people. They moved inland to "Free China," the area where the Japanese had not yet penetrated, and began their missionary work there.

With all this going on around her, Betty began to feel she should be doing something more than just filing papers and typing letters for her father. She went to discuss the matter with an old friend of the family, Mrs. Bowman. She knocked on the painted wooden door, and a minute later Mrs. Bowman opened it. Her twinkling blue eyes lit up when she saw Betty. "Come in, my dear," she said, beaming. "I was just having a cup of coffee. Won't you join me?"

"Thank you very much," Betty replied, kissing the seventy-year-old woman on the cheek.

Over coffee all of Betty's frustrations poured out. Betty knew what she didn't want to do for a job, but she couldn't work out what it was she wanted to do.

"I always think God plants His desires in our hearts so we will act on them," Mrs. Bowman said, placing her coffee cup on the end table between the two of them. "What is it you love to do the most?"

Betty hesitated for a moment. "I like to fly," she said, then added hastily, "but I know that on my income that's a frivolous waste."

"Umm," Mrs. Bowman replied, her bushy white eyebrows rising. "And what else do you like?"

Betty thought again. "Well, I love helping to run the youth group at church," she said.

"Do you think God might have given you both of these interests for a reason? Perhaps you should think of combining them and using flying for some Christian missions work."

Betty hardly heard another word Mrs. Bowman said. It was as if the old woman had jolted her with an electric shock. Why hadn't she thought of it herself? Flying and missionary work—it would be a dream come true! But was it possible? Did God really want her to do the thing she wanted to do most?

As Betty left Mrs. Bowman's home, she prayed silently. "God, I've never heard of anyone who used flying to help spread the gospel message, but if You want me to fly for You, show me how to make it happen."

As she walked home down the gravel road, Betty's heart raced with excitement. God was in control of her future, and He would make things work out for good for her.

Within several weeks of her visit with Mrs. Bowman, Betty heard of a civilian pilot training course offered by the University of Washington. Although the United States was not officially at war, the country was gearing up for the possibility. As a result, many young pilots were being trained. There was, however, a lot of debate about the value of training women pilots. After all, a woman could never be expected to fly an airplane in combat!

Betty had expected it would be difficult convincing her parents to allow her to enroll in the course, but she was in for a surprise. Her parents told her that since she had tried her hardest to fit in as a nurse and it had not worked, they were willing to support her in whatever she decided to do. In 1941 Betty Greene was accepted into the pilot training course. She was one of three women in a class of forty.

The course was a dream come true. On Lake Washington, she spent hours practicing landing and taking off in a float plane, often flying right over the new house her parents had finally been able to build to replace the one that had burned down thirteen years before. Betty loved the smooth feel of the float plane beneath her. She loved to see the powerful jets of water spraying behind her as she pulled back on the joystick and the plane lifted off the surface of the lake.

Betty passed the course with honors, gaining her private pilot's license with ratings to fly both regular and float planes. After the pilot training course ended, however, it didn't seem to Betty that she was any closer to a new career. There were no openings for women in the military. Her parents urged her to finish college. Betty thought this was a good idea, only this time she chose classes she liked instead of nursing. This time around, school was a pleasure, especially the classes in which she learned about how people in other parts of the world thought and lived. In June 1942, Betty graduated with a bachelor of arts in sociology (her nursing courses applied toward her degree), with special studies in various world cultures.

Just before graduating, Betty had read a newspaper article about a group of women pilots that was being formed to serve in the military. The women would not go into combat themselves but would ferry planes back and forth and undertake other flying tasks to release male pilots to fly combat missions. Betty didn't say anything to anyone about what she'd read. Instead she prayed that God would show her whether this was the right step for her to take.

A week later she got her answer. Her parents returned home suspiciously late after a day in Seattle. As her mother removed her hat and gloves and rearranged her hair, she smiled at Betty. "Your father and I have something to tell you," she said, clearing her throat.

Betty looked at her father with a questioning glance. "What?" she asked.

"Today we went to see a Mrs. Ethel Sheehy."

Betty gasped. She recognized the name immediately. Mrs. Sheehy was the woman mentioned in the article in the newspaper. "Why?" she finally responded, hoping she already knew the answer.

"Well, we read an article about the Women's Flying Training Detachment, and we wanted to learn more about it."

"And?" Betty prodded.

"It sounds like a fine idea," grinned her father. "Mrs. Sheehy would like to meet you. Here's the phone number of her hotel. She's in room 357. You go and meet with her and hear for yourself what she has to say."

Betty hugged her parents. "Thank you, thank you so much," she said.

Later that week Betty met with Mrs. Sheehy and learned that her private pilot's license was enough to qualify her for enrollment into the program. Only women between the ages of twenty-one and thirty-four were being considered, so at twenty-two, Betty would be one of the youngest applicants.

In February 1943, Betty received an official letter from Jacqueline Cochran, a whirlwind of a woman who had founded a successful cosmetics company before taking to the air and winning many flying races, including the Bendix Transcontinental Air Race. When America entered the war after the Pearl Harbor bombing on December 7, 1941, Jacqueline Cochran had put all of this aside to concentrate on ways in which women pilots could be used to ease the burden on male pilots. She enlisted the help of General "Hap" Arnold, and together they formed the Women's Flying Training Detachment (WFTD). In her letter, Jacqueline Cochran advised Betty, "Upon clearance of your Civil Service appointment and approval of your medical examination, you will be officially notified when and where to report for duty." She also asked Betty not to publicize the fact that she was going to be a pilot in the war effort. No one wanted to give the Japanese or the Germans the idea that America had become so desperate it had stooped to using women to fly airplanes!

If it was hard for Albert and Gertrude Greene in March 1943 to say farewell to their only daughter, they did not show it. Betty was the last of their children to leave home. Her oldest brother, Joe, was now a Baptist pastor, while Al and Thelma and their new son, Norman, were still in China. Because of the war, no one had heard from them in over a year. Meanwhile, Betty's twin brother, Bill, was an up-and-coming lieutenant with the army in the Coast Artillery. After completing his officers' training, he'd been too young to immediately be commissioned with the rest of his class. His fellow classmates had been dispatched to fight in the Philippines, where many of them had died defending the island fortress of Corregidor in Manila Bay or on the "Death March" the Japanese had forced their American captives to make along the Bataan Peninsula. Bill already knew more people who had been killed in the war than all the children he'd known at Hunts Point Elementary School growing up.

Three smaller groups of women pilots had been trained at a facility in Houston, Texas, but this time around, a larger group of women was to take over the men's flight training facility at Avenger Field in Sweetwater, Texas. Betty was advised she would be part of this group, and she made her way to Sweetwater, about forty miles west of Abilene.

Betty arrived at Avenger Field on a cool March morning along with over one hundred other women pilots. Each woman was assigned to a sleeping area, or "bay," as it was called. In each bay were set up six cots, along with desks, chairs, and lockers. Between every two bays was a single bathroom. Betty rolled her eyes when she saw the housing arrangements. Some of the women pilots she'd seen looked as though it took them half an hour just to get their hair right. This could make for some long lines waiting to use the bathroom.

After they had unpacked their bags into the pineboard lockers beside their cots, the women were told to change into uniform and report for duty. This was where the first problem arose. There were no women's uniforms, only some oversized olive green coveralls left by the men who had been trained at the base before them. Since there was nothing else to change into, the "zoot suits," as the coveralls came to be known, had to do.

At 1 P.M. Betty Greene found herself lined up with 130 other women from all forty-eight states. Being taller than most of the others meant she was placed near the back of the line. It also meant she was one of the few women whose zoot suit almost fit her—in length anyway. Lined up in front of her was a particularly short woman. The crotch of this woman's coveralls, which were about two sizes larger than Betty's, hung down past her knees, making it impossible for her to walk without looking like a penguin. The legs of her zoot suit had been rolled up so many times she had to walk with her legs wide apart to avoid tripping over the wad of fabric. Betty noticed many of the other women smirking as they watched this woman. Indeed, she had to admit it did look comical. Still, Betty felt sorry for the woman and decided she would swap coveralls with her. Betty's coveralls would at least be a little smaller, making it easier for the woman to get around.

"Attention, class 43-W-5," yelled a male officer with crewcut hair and large rubbery ears that stuck straight out from the side of his head. "In line. Hup to!"

The women looked at one another, and Betty wanted to laugh out loud. It was like being in a Laurel and Hardy movie, and she thought for sure the officer was trying to impress the women. When he turned, she saw the serious look on his face. It was a look that told them all they were now on an air base and they had better follow orders, or else.

The women were told to march into an empty hangar, where their commanding officer introduced himself. Then he barked, "Look to your right and your left." Betty took that as an order and looked around. "Only one in three of you is going to graduate from this program," he continued. "That is, two out of every three of you will be dropouts, failures. Be the one who makes it. Be diligent." With that he turned and marched away.

Betty was left standing at attention in the hangar with the other women in their comically oversized coveralls, wondering what she had gotten herself into, and what would happen next.

Chapter 4

An Eager Learner

Betty need not have worried about the amount of time the women in her bay would spend in the single bathroom. They were all kept so busy that when they got back to their bay at ten in the evening, all they could do was collapse onto their cots exhausted. And they would groan as they rolled out of bed when reveille sounded at six o'clock the following morning. Before long, they all sported "PT (pilot training) suntans," deep brown tans from spending hours on end in the sun, except for the raccoonlike pale rings around their eyes from the goggles they wore during training.

After breakfast, roll call, and barracks inspection, the remainder of the morning was spent in flying practice and instruction. During the afternoon and evening, they spent time marching on the drill field, competing on the obstacle course, and using the Link trainer, a simple flight simulator that allowed pilots to pitch and turn in response to the way they moved the control stick. On top of all these activities, the women spent five hours a day studying math, physics, meteorology, aerodynamics, electronics, navigation, military and civilian air regulations, and engine operation and maintenance. Each subject required a heavy workload, not to mention lots of tests. Along with the others in the Women's Flying Training Detachment, Betty found herself studying during every spare moment she had.

Although the women were stationed on a military base and were treated as if they were in the army, technically they were not. They were all volunteers, and this led to some important distinctions between them and the men in the army. For one thing, they were not bonded to the military and could quit at any time. They were also required to pay for their own uniforms, and Betty, along with the others, handed over $100 for her cap, goggles, jacket, and parachute. And unlike the men, the women had to pay the army for their room and board, which cost $1.65 a day. This daily amount was deducted from the $150 they were paid each month.

Many of the women complained about the unfairness of the system, but Betty didn't care. She had her sights set on something more important than what she was doing right then. She intended to learn as much as possible, get all the flying experience she could, and when the war was over somehow use it all to help with missionary work.

The experience she gained at Avenger Field was more than she could have hoped for. Within two weeks of arrival she was flying solo in a PT-19A, a 175-horsepower open-cockpit training airplane that cruised along at ninety miles per hour. Her instructor insisted she double-check her safety belt before each takeoff, and it was not long before Betty learned how important his advice was. One morning as she stood in line waiting for her turn to fly and memorizing a page from her navigational textbook, a PT-19A taxied down the runway. As Betty glanced up at it, she did a double take. The instructor was sitting in the rear cockpit seat, but the front cockpit was empty! The woman who had gone up in the plane just fifteen minutes before had vanished. Only the earphones dangling over the edge of the cockpit gave any hint she had been there.

Betty looked around in a panic. Other women gasped at the sight. What had happened to their fellow pilot? The instructor climbed out of the airplane and jumped to the ground. "It's always a good idea to double-check your safety belt," he said dryly. "This woman didn't, and she fell out while doing a spin."

Betty's heart raced. This could have happened to any of them.

"The good thing is, she kept her wits about her and remembered to pull the ripcord on her parachute.

She'll be fine," the instructor added, obviously enjoying the shock and suspense he had created.

The pilot was fine, just as the instructor had said. But it was only a few weeks later that another incident occurred, and this time it did not have such a happy ending. The basic training phase of their program had finished, and the women had moved on to instrument and night flying. One woman from Betty's bay was scheduled for a night flying session. After dinner she climbed into a BT-13 aircraft. Betty happened to be walking by and listened as the 450-horsepower engine throbbed into motion. Everything sounded normal, and Betty did not give it a second thought. However, the plane never returned to Avenger Field, and its burned wreckage was found in a cattle pasture at daybreak the following morning. Both the instructor and the pilot were killed in the crash.

As a result of the accident, Betty vowed to be even more careful while flying and to diligently keep her eyes on the goal of learning all she could about flying aircraft under various conditions. She also thought more about missionary work and how her flying might help. One day she decided to write down her thoughts on the subject and submit them to *Power*, a magazine for teenagers published by Scripture Union Press.

Betty thought for a long time about what to say and in the end started her article with a brief description of what she did each day. She followed it by saying: "Why do I want to fly? Probably for the same reason hundreds of you would like to, but mainly because I am looking forward to being a missionary and think flying is going to be very useful in the work of spreading the message of Christ...."

The article was published along with a photo of Betty in her olive-green coveralls. Little did she know that these words would begin a chain of events that would define the rest of her life. An editor from *His*, InterVarsity Christian Fellowship's magazine, read her article and asked her to write an article for the magazine about what she hoped to do when the war was over. The article was published in late spring 1943.

As the hot West Texas summer settled over Avenger Field, the pace of training heated up. By now the women had advanced to flying the AT-6 Texan, an advanced single-engine training airplane. It was the first plane Betty had flown with retractable landing gear, and its six-hundred-horsepower engine allowed her to cruise along at 145 miles per hour. Betty loved the throb of the powerful engine and practiced landings and takeoffs until she could do them perfectly every time.

The threat of an unsatisfactory test flight hung over Betty as it did all the women in the training program. When a pilot performed an unsatisfactory test flight, she was handed a pink form with a large "U" for unsatisfactory stamped across it. The pilot was then given a second chance to prove she could perform the particular procedure. This flight was called the E-ride. The "E" stood for elimination. If a pilot failed the second test, she was dismissed from the program and within a few hours had packed her belongings and left the base. At times Betty and her fellow pilots would line up for roll call, only to find someone was not there. The pilot had washed out on the E-ride and left, too humiliated to even say good-bye. This created a constant tension on base: Exams had to be passed in all subjects, and every flying technique had to be perfected in only six months.

With all the work involved, time flew by, and before Betty knew it, it was September 1943, and graduation. Graduation day was particularly hot, so hot that the tarmac stuck to Betty's boots as she marched in formation to the quadrangle. She, like all the other eighty-five graduating pilots, was dressed in the unofficial Women's Flying Training Detachment uniform—wide-legged khaki pants, short-sleeved white shirt, and khaki boatcap. The band struck up as class 43-W-5 stood to attention for inspection.

Keeping her head facing forward and as motionless as possible, Betty scanned the makeshift bleachers to her right and left. She knew many of the other women had their parents and siblings in the crowd, but Betty's family was not there. It surprised her to feel a lump in her throat. She had been so busy with her final exams that she hadn't had time to think about what graduation would be like without anyone she loved looking on.

Soon the speeches began. Captain Elmer Riley, the flight school director, stood to praise those who had made it through the program. He talked about how reliable the women were, how he thought they worked harder and were more responsible than the men, especially when it came to buzzing the nearby towns in their airplanes! Everyone laughed. Jacqueline Cochran was the last person to speak. She told the women pilots how proud she was of them and pointed out that although they could have left at any time, only 42 of the original 130 women had washed out. This was a one-third dropout rate, no higher than the men, who did not have the choice of leaving simply because they'd had enough.

The sun continued to beat down as Jacqueline Cochran finished her speech. Then as each woman's name was called, the women walked up the concrete ramp to the dais to receive their wings and diploma. Jacqueline Cochran welcomed each of them as a fully fledged WASP, or member of the Women Airforce Service Pilots, as the Women's Flying Training Detachment was now called.

As the silver wings with W 5 on a shield in the center were pinned onto her shirt, Betty thought about the future. She and two of her roommates, Ann Baumgartner, who would go on to become the first woman to fly a jet airplane, and Carol Jones, had been posted to Camp Davis in North Carolina. It was not until the three of them had arrived at Camp Davis a week later that they learned why they had been sent there. In July twenty-five Women Airforce Service Pilots from the previous class in Houston had been assigned to the camp. Betty was being added to the group as an extra pilot, while Ann Baumgartner and Carol Jones were replacing two of the WASPs who had been killed in flying accidents. Jacqueline Cochran had investigated both crashes, and although her report was classified, rumor was that sugar had been found in at least one of the crashed airplanes' fuel tanks. Most people thought there was probably a man or group of men on base who resented the idea of using women pilots, though no one was ever charged with sabotage.

Upon their arrival at Camp Davis, the three women were allowed thirty minutes to settle in before they had to report for their first briefing. The room they were assigned to was much like the one at Avenger Field, and Betty guessed that the rooms were probably the same on every military base across the United States.

Betty was putting her clothes in a locker when she glanced out the window. Two men were walking past the barracks. One was short and blond. The other was tall and had reddish brown hair. Betty's mouth dropped open when she saw him. She dashed out the door to catch up with the men. She could hardly believe her eyes. "Bill!" she yelled. "What on earth are you doing here?"

The tall man turned to look at her, a stunned look on his face as he laid eyes on his twin sister. Betty had only a few minutes to question him, but she found out that Bill had just been assigned to Camp Davis for an officers' antiaircraft gunnery course. The two of them promised to find each other at dinner that night, and with a huge smile on her face, Betty hurried off to join Ann Baumgartner and Carol Jones for their briefing.

Before the end of the day, Betty knew exactly what her job was going to entail. The job had three parts, all aimed at giving the men on the base ways to practice fighting aircraft. The first part of the job required Betty to fly her plane along specially coded routes while radar operators on the ground tracked the plane so they could give its exact location at any given moment. The second part of the job involved flying over the base at night, allowing the men to practice their searchlight techniques and get the feel for how to spotlight enemy aircraft flying overhead under the cover of darkness. It was the third part of the job that boggled Betty's mind the most. She would pull a large fabric target behind her plane while the men on the ground who were training to use antiaircraft guns would practice their aim by shooting at the target. This target practice sounded fine until Betty learned they would be using live ammunition. She only hoped their aim was good.

Chapter 5

Higher Than She'd Ever Been Before

Betty's first target-towing flight turned out to be more eventful than she could have imagined. After taking off in a Lockheed B-34 bomber, a large canvas target flapping on the end of a cable behind the plane, Betty climbed to two thousand feet. As she did so, a male officer sent to check her out on her first flight in the aircraft dozed in the copilot's seat beside her. Betty wasn't sure whether his actions showed complete confidence in her flying ability or complete contempt for her as a woman pilot. She suspected the latter, as most of the men at Camp Davis seemed to resent the women pilots of the WASP.

At two thousand feet, Betty leveled off the airplane. As she proceeded to make a pass over the gunnery range where the antiaircraft gunners were practicing, shells began to burst around the Lockheed bomber. Betty was frightened. This was her first flight towing a target, and she had no idea whether or not this was normal. As she was debating whether to wake the officer sleeping next to her and ask him whether or not it was normal, a shell exploded so close to the plane that in a split second, the officer went from sleeping to sitting bolt upright.

"What was that?" he yelled.

"Shells are exploding all around us. Is that normal?" Betty asked.

"Normal, normal!" the officer spluttered. "Some fool down there is aiming right at us and not the target! What are they trying to do, shoot us down?" With that he began barking orders over the radio to the ground, and soon the shelling stopped.

Betty made several more runs over the antiaircraft gunnery range, but they were less eventful, with the gunners this time aiming and shooting at the canvas target trailing behind the Lockheed bomber.

The weeks rolled by, and although Betty had no more close calls, she was always careful when she flew. Her superiors must have taken note, because early one morning in January 1944, a messenger arrived at Betty's barracks.

"I have orders for Elizabeth Greene," the messenger said, handing Betty an official-looking envelope.

Betty thanked the messenger and sat down to read the orders. She was being reassigned to Wright

Field in Dayton, Ohio, to be involved in the aeronautical research division. Betty laid the orders down and wondered what aeronautical research might be. She had no idea. As she pondered, her friend Ann Baumgartner burst into the room.

"Guess what?" she said gloomily.

"What?" Betty asked.

"I've just been reassigned to Wright Field in Ohio," she said, waving a copy of her orders at Betty.

Betty laughed and showed Ann her own orders. "So have I," she said.

The two women burst into laughter.

"Well, if we're going together, it won't be too bad. What do you think we'll be doing there? It all sounds very secretive, doesn't it?" Ann said.

"It sure does. We'll just have to wait and find out, I guess," Betty said.

Ten days later, Betty and Ann arrived at the Miami Hotel in Dayton, Ohio. They spent a restful night there and in the morning were met by Major Frederick Borsodi, a tall, dark-haired man who escorted them by car to Wright Field. As they rode, Major Borsodi chatted to them about some of the work he was doing at the air base. His area of expertise encompassed learning about compression shock waves on the wings of airplanes. Major Borsodi was the first man to see these and the first to photograph them. He told Betty that to do this he had put a P-51D aircraft into a dive from forty thousand feet.

Betty was impressed. The highest she had ever flown herself was nineteen thousand feet, and anything over twenty-five thousand feet was considered dangerous—for three reasons. First, the lack of oxygen at such high altitudes caused hypoxia, which made pilots feel peaceful and sluggish. As a result, their judgment was impaired, and if they didn't get to a lower altitude and more oxygen fast, they could drift into unconsciousness and death. Second was the problem of extreme cold at such heights. The temperature could go down to minus eighty degrees Fahrenheit, or even lower. At such temperatures, a person would be instantly frostbitten. Third was the threat of an embolism. What happened to pilots at such an altitude was similar to what happened to deep-sea divers who resurfaced too quickly: They got the bends. Basically, the fast reduction in atmospheric pressure caused gas bubbles to form in the blood. These bubbles were mostly nitrogen and made a person feel itchy, suffer blurred vision, and then become paralyzed and die.

Major Borsodi explained that a big problem for the United States in the war was that German airplanes could fly higher than Allied planes and were bombing them from higher altitudes. At Wright Field, the Americans were experimenting with high-altitude flying, because the side that developed airplanes that could fly higher than all others would have a definite advantage in the air.

By the time the Pontiac carrying Major Borsodi, Betty, and Ann pulled into Wright Field, Betty was beginning to wonder what she had let herself in for.

Was *she* going to be flying at such heights? Or did the air force have something else in mind for her?

Betty did not have to wait long to find out. A note was on the message board when she arrived asking her and Ann to report immediately to Colonel Randolph Lovelace II, M.D., director of the Aeromedical Laboratory. Betty straightened her bun and set out with Ann Baumgartner to find Colonel Lovelace.

The colonel turned out to be a kindly man of medium height and build, with his left hand heavily bandaged. "Ah, ladies, I have been waiting to meet you," he said in a pleasant voice, inviting them into his large office. "Please sit down, and I'll try to fill you in on why you are here."

Betty and Ann sat in comfortable overstuffed easy chairs and peered across the desk at the colonel.

Colonel Lovelace cleared his throat. "Welcome to Wright Field. I'm glad to have two WASPs on my staff. I think you can make a valuable contribution to the work we're doing here."

Betty smiled. "Just what work is that?" she asked politely.

Colonel Lovelace grinned. "Very cutting-edge work," he replied. "Let me tell you about it."

Over the next hour, the colonel laid out the work he had been involved in and the strides he had made since the beginning of the war. In 1940 a strato-chamber had been invented to simulate conditions at forty thousand feet. This meant that for the first time, the responses of the human body to high altitudes could be studied without the risk of actually being in the stratosphere. By 1943 much work had been done on radio communications, making it possible for aircraft to transmit radio messages from forty thousand feet. Now the research team had turned its attention to making and testing oxygen masks and flight suits that would allow pilots to fly at thirty-five thousand feet and higher for long periods.

Betty Greene and Ann Baumgartner were to be a part of the team that would be the first to test the new equipment. "Though, of course," Colonel Lovelace added, "I never ask my men or women to do anything I have not done myself."

Betty did not fully understand how serious the colonel was about this until later that night in the mess hall. Over a bowl of beef stew and biscuits, she learned from one of the men on base that Colonel Lovelace had been the second person to ever jump from an airplane flying in the stratosphere. The colonel had jumped from seven and one-half miles up in an attempt to determine whether a parachutist could survive a drop from that height. He had jumped using a tethered line to activate his parachute in case he became unconscious. It was a good thing he had, because the jolt of the parachute opening had hit him with a force of six Gs, knocking him unconscious. As he fell silently through the near oxygenless atmosphere, his left glove slipped off, exposing his hand to minus sixty degrees Fahrenheit. An oxygen bottle strapped to the inside of his right leg supplied him with air to breathe as he fell. He had plummeted thirty-four hundred feet before he regained consciousness and pulled his exposed hand into his sleeve. Colonel Lovelace had landed safely in a wheat field. He was rushed off to the hospital to treat his frostbitten hand.

"So that explains the bandages," Betty said to Ann as they walked back to their new barracks for the night.

The next morning their work began. Betty and Ann were fitted with oxygen masks and began preparations for an eventual flight into the stratosphere aboard a modified four-engine Boeing B-17 Flying Fortress bomber. They spent hours each day in the strato-chamber discovering the tolerances and limits of their bodies under various stresses.

By the end of the week, they had their first experience of high-altitude flying. Betty loved everything about it, especially the deep-blue color of the sky and the almost endless vista of land below them. They had been maintaining an altitude of thirty-five thousand feet for about an hour and a half when one of the officers scribbled a note and handed it to Betty, who grabbed it with her heavy fur-lined glove. "Prepare for immediate descent. Pass it on," the note read. Betty passed the note to Ann. As Betty pulled her safety belt to its tightest setting, she wondered what the problem could be. Seconds later, the B-17 went into a steep dive. In less than five minutes it had dropped twenty thousand feet to a safer altitude of fifteen thousand feet.

It was not until the plane had safely landed that Betty found out the full story. One of the airmen had accidentally disconnected his oxygen line, and by the time the problem was discovered, he was unconscious. No one knew whether there was time to save him, but the plane had dived as steeply as it could. By the grace of God, the airman had regained consciousness and made a full recovery. Although the incident had ended well, it made Betty vow to be extra careful. One wrong move at such altitudes could easily cost her her life.

Several days later, Betty, along with Ann Baumgartner and some airmen, was conducting tests using electrified flying suits to see how warm people could stay. There was only one way to find out. When the B-17 reached forty thousand feet, the windows were wound down and the doors rolled back. Frigid air rushed into the plane, biting at Betty's face mask. Betty pulled her legs up under her chin and sat still, watching the young gunner opposite her who was conducting tests to see how weapons operated in such sub-zero temperatures. The gunner struggled to load the gun, the heavy gloves and extreme cold making it nearly impossible to move the ammunition into position. In the end, he just shrugged at Betty and laid the weapon aside. It was impossible to use it under such conditions.

Next Betty's attention was drawn to the lieutenant monitoring them all. He moved silently from one person to the next, checking their oxygen levels and intake valves. For some reason, Betty glanced down at her own oxygen gauge. To her horror, the needle was on zero. No oxygen was getting through to her!

For a split second, Betty wanted to panic. Without oxygen she would be unconscious within thirty seconds. But thinking quickly, she waved her arms to get the lieutenant's attention. She pointed to her oxygen tank as he hurried over. She held her breath while the lieutenant felt his way down her intake tube. About a third of the way along, he looked up and then began massaging the tube. Betty knew immediately what had happened. The flexible hose had become blocked with ice that had formed from the condensation of her warm breath. She reached down to help, and the ice blockage was soon cleared. Life-sustaining oxygen flowed into her oxygen mask, and Betty gave the lieutenant a thumbs-up.

Not everyone survived the tests. A few days later, a colonel made a parachute jump from forty thousand feet. He did not use a tethered line to automatically open his chute, since he was experimenting with opening his own parachute. He blacked out soon after jumping from the airplane and plummeted to the ground, his unopened parachute strapped uselessly to his back. Days later, a pilot was diving his P-38 airplane from high altitude and was unable to regain control and pull out of the dive. The plane slammed into the ground, killing the pilot.

Of course, everyone knew there were dangers involved in performing the tests. But Betty, like the others serving at Wright Field, was willing to accept the risk. It was mid-1944, and the war had reached an important phase. The Allies were preparing for a massive invasion of France to defeat the occupying German forces there and needed every tactical advantage they could muster. So despite the ever present danger, Betty happily threw herself into the work. As she did so, life at Wright Field seemed to fall into a routine for her.

Chapter 6

You Are Not Alone

Betty stood back from those still waiting for their name to be called and glanced at the two letters she had received. One was from her mother, but she did not recognize the handwriting on the other one. It was postmarked Floyd Bennett Field, N.Y., and was dated July 1, 1944. It had taken only a week to reach her. Not bad for wartime, she mused to herself as she tore the envelope open and unfolded the neat handwritten pages it contained. She began to read. "Dear Miss Greene, I read your article in last year's spring issue of *His* magazine and wanted to inform you that you are not alone. There are several others of us who share your vision for using aircraft and pilots to spread the gospel to the ends of the earth."

Betty's heart raced as she walked briskly back to her barracks. This was the kind of letter a person needed time to digest without interruptions. She sat down on the edge of her cot and continued reading. The letter went on to say that three men, Jim Truxton, who was writing the letter, Jim Buyers, and "Soddy" (Clarence) Soderberg, had been meeting together for over a year to pray for and plan an organization that would use military-trained pilots to help support missionaries when the war was over. Betty could hardly believe what she was reading. This was exactly the thing she had hoped to become a part of when the war ended!

Betty read eagerly on. Since the war was dragging on, the new organization the men hoped to start had no staff, but it did have a name. It was called the Christian Airmen's Missionary Fellowship, or CAMF for short. In light of Betty's article about using her flying skills to serve God, Jim Truxton wondered whether Betty might be able to come to Washington, D.C., sometime soon to meet him and talk more about the plans for CAMF. Betty wrote straight back to Jim to tell him she would keep her eyes and ears open for a way to get to Washington, D.C.

Two weeks later, Betty checked the assignment board and found she had been ordered to report to Jacqueline Cochran at her office in the Pentagon. Some important papers were to be hand-delivered to Avenger Field in Sweetwater, Texas. Somehow Betty had been given the task. She was delighted. This meant she would be able to meet with Jim Truxton in Washington sooner than she'd thought.

The WASP office in the Pentagon was deep in the heart of the building at the end of a long string of corridors. Jacqueline Cochran was warm and welcoming, and Betty chatted with her awhile before collecting the papers to be delivered and heading back to the Shoreham Hotel, where she would be staying for the night before flying out first thing in the morning.

That evening Betty had dinner in the hotel dining room with Jim Truxton, who had traveled to Washington to meet her on a special twenty-four-hour leave from Floyd Bennett Field in New York. Betty sized Jim up. Jim Truxton was her height and had clear blue eyes and brown wavy hair set back on a high forehead. Betty decided he must be about thirty, five years older than she was. His face was creased with a permanent smile, and she liked him from the start. Over dinner Jim told her more about himself and his work as a navy pilot. He was assigned to a duty he loved, protecting large convoys of thirty to fifty ships crossing the Atlantic Ocean from New York to England. The ships carried vital supplies to keep Great Britain's war effort going. Because of this, many German submarines prowled the ocean waiting to torpedo and sink the ships. Jim Truxton's job was to shadow the convoys in his Martin Mariner Seaplane, spot the submarines, and drop depth charges on them.

As dessert arrived, Jim Truxton began to unfold his vision for CAMF to Betty. By the time the evening was over, Betty had promised to pray about becoming involved with the group once the war was over.

A month later, in August 1944, Betty received a follow-up letter from Jim Truxton asking her if she would be willing to open CAMF's first office in Los Angeles. Betty thought about it for a long time. As a WASP, she was officially a volunteer, which meant that unlike enlisted men such as Jim Truxton, she could quit anytime she wanted. Being a woman pilot made her the only "airman" who could actually begin the work of CAMF while the war was still in progress. But Betty was not a quitter. She loved her flying work, especially since she knew it was helping America's war effort. In the end, she decided not to leave the WASP to start CAMF's first office. Instead she decided to wait until God opened the door for her to work with CAMF.

A week later, Betty received news she could never have predicted. She was asked to copilot a C-60 Lodestar airplane to Tampa, Florida, to be used for paratroopers to practice jumping into the waters of the Gulf of Mexico. The first leg of the flight from Wright Field to Atlanta went without a hitch. It was after she had landed in Atlanta that Betty received the surprising news.

A short, blond woman in a WASP uniform ran up to her as she prepared the plane for refueling. "Have you heard the news?" the woman asked.

"What news?" Betty asked, thinking the woman may have confused her with someone else.

"About the WASP," the woman replied. "We're being disbanded!"

"Disbanded?" Betty echoed, unsure whether she had heard right.

"Yes, disbanded," the woman replied. "There isn't a date set yet, but they say it's going to happen before Christmas."

"But why would the government disband the WASP before the war is over?" Betty asked, trying to understand the news.

"General Arnold says the work the WASP does is going to become part of the Army Air Force. And of course, the kicker is, women can't be in the military. So we're all going to be dumped."

Betty's heart sank. Was her "military" career about to come to a premature end after all?

The question lingered in her mind as she completed the second leg of the flight to Tampa and as she flew across the Gulf of Mexico dropping paratroopers dressed in full combat gear over the deep blue waters.

When Betty got back to Wright Field two days later, the news was official. It came in the form of a letter from Jacqueline Cochran addressed to all WASP personnel. Betty's heart sank as she read it. "The Army Air Force will issue a certificate of honorable service and discharge similar to the type issued to officers when they are relieved from active duty. In addition, you will receive a card designating you as a rated pilot of military aircraft indicating the horsepower rating for which you are qualified. These cards can be used as a basis to obtain a CAA commercial license in the same manner as do male military pilots.... Those who wish to continue to fly for the Army Air Force will be disappointed, but no WASP familiar with the pertinent facts would question the decision or its time limits...."

As if that were not blunt enough, there was also a letter from General H. Arnold. It read, "The WASP became part of the Army Air Force in order to release male pilots for other duties. Their very successful record of accomplishments has proved that in any future total effort the nation can count on thousands of its young women to fly any of its aircraft. You have freed male pilots for other work, but now the war situation has changed and the time has come when your volunteered services are no longer needed. The situation is that if you continue to serve, you will be replacing instead of releasing our young men. I know that the WASP wouldn't want that. So I have directed that the WASP program be inactivated and all WASP be released by 20 December 1944."

Gradually the "pertinent facts" Jacqueline Cochran referred to in her letter began to filter down to the women. A bill to militarize women pilots and allow them to serve as enlisted women had been defeated in Congress in June 1944. The bill had failed mostly because of the lobbying efforts of a group of male civilian flight instructors who had been hired by the Army Air Force as flight trainers. As such they were exempt from being drafted to go overseas and fight. However, by now the final outcome of the war seemed certain, and the need to train new pilots began to taper off. The United States now had more than enough trained pilots. With no more pilots to train, the male civilian flight trainers would be drafted and sent off to fight. To avoid this, they needed to come up with some other essential unenlisted flying tasks. Their solution was to take over the WASP jobs and keep themselves and their civilian salaries safe at home.

When they discovered the truth, many of the women were upset. They had risked their lives alongside the men, only to be thrown aside when it suited the powers that be. And when they applied for jobs as commercial pilots, they were offered positions as stewardesses. They were told the "real" flying jobs were being held open for male pilots when they returned home from the war.

Betty was offered a nonenlisted secretarial job in the Army Air Force, which she turned down. She had joined the WASP to use her flying skills, not her office skills, to help the war effort. And now it seemed her flying services were no longer needed. As her days of flying military aircraft wound down, Betty was not bitter, as were so many of her colleagues. All along she had been preparing to put her flying skills to work in another direction.

Betty had accumulated extra leave time, so in early October 1944, she began packing her bag for the train trip back to Evergreen Point, Washington, to visit her parents, whom she hadn't seen in eighteen months.

Three days before she was due to leave, a good friend and fellow pilot asked her if she would fly a new experimental plane with him to Baltimore. She was torn between wanting to get home to her parents and taking one last flight, especially in a new airplane. In the end she told her friend she would go with him if he could not find anyone else to go along.

Her friend did not call her back, so Betty assumed he had found someone else to copilot the airplane. Two days later, the solemn news was delivered to the assembled crowd in the mess hall. The plane had taken off from Baltimore on a return flight to Wright Field, but after only three minutes in the air it exploded in a huge fireball. All those aboard—Betty's pilot friend, the general in charge of helicopter development at Wright Field, an operations officer, and a three-man crew—were killed.

That evening was Betty's last night as a WASP, and she took a long walk in the cool fall air. She was saddened by the news she'd just heard, and relieved that once again she had narrowly escaped death. She could easily have been copilot on the doomed flight. As the moon shone down, lighting her path, she had a strange feeling that the unseen hand of God was guiding her and that He would continue to guide her in the dangerous situations she was sure lay ahead as she sought to put her flying experience to work helping to spread the gospel around the world.

Chapter 7

Getting Started

It was a cold, wet night on October 30, 1944, when Betty Greene stepped off the train in Seattle and into the arms of her father. It was a wonderful reunion—everything Betty had dreamed it would be since she had learned the WASP would be disbanded. Her older brothers Joe and Al were there, too, along with their wives and an ever growing brood of nieces and nephews. Betty loved being back in the midst of her family, but from the outset she told them she was home only to visit, not to stay. Another mission awaited her. She was going to help the Christian Airmen's Missionary Fellowship get started so that when the war finally ended, Christian pilots would have a way to use their flying talents for missions.

Six weeks later Betty was on another train, this time headed for Los Angeles, California. After living in the wonderful natural surrounding of home—the tall evergreen trees and the deep green waters of Lake Washington—she found it hard to imagine settling into a large, sprawling city like Los Angeles. But Los Angeles was where Jim Truxton had arranged for CAMF's headquarters to be situated. He had chosen Los Angeles because of a generous offer from a man named Dawson Trotman. In 1933 Dawson Trotman and his young wife, Lila, had moved to Long Beach, California, to share the gospel message and open their home to sailors. This vision for evangelism had led to their running a number of Bible study groups and the development of a Bible memorization system known as the Navigators. Dawson Trotman had named his ministry after the Bible memorization system.

When the war broke out, the Navigators system became very popular with Christian servicemen. Soon nearly every ship and military base had a group of eager young Christian men meeting together to study and memorize the Bible and encourage one another. To keep in contact with these men, the Navigators published a newsletter called *The Log*, which was sent to thousands of Christian soldiers, sailors, and pilots on a regular basis.

Jim Truxton had written several letters to Betty about Dawson Trotman. Although the two men had met only briefly once, Dawson Trotman was an eager supporter of the fledgling CAMF. He promised to do all he could to help get the new organization started, including offering free office space and a room in his home where Betty could stay while she got established in Los Angeles.

Dawson Trotman picked Betty up at the train station and drove her through tree-lined streets to his home. Nothing could have prepared Betty for the house she was going to be staying in. She had just finished thanking Dawson for his generous offer of a room, adding that she hoped her staying there wouldn't make the house too crowded, when the 1941 Oldsmobile coupe they were riding in turned into the driveway of house number 509. As she gazed up at the fifty-year-old house, Betty chuckled to herself. There was enough room for her and about forty others in the house—a two-story mansion with a full attic. The house had twin turrets and a huge verandah that ran the length of the house.

As they walked up the front path, which wound its way past several stately magnolia trees, Dawson Trotman explained that the Fuller Evangelistic Foundation actually owned the house and rented it to the Navigators at a fraction of its worth. It was Charles Fuller's way of supporting the work of Dawson and Lila Trotman and the Navigators.

Dawson Trotman opened the huge leaded-glass front door for Betty. The house echoed with laughter and overflowed with interesting people. Dawson and Lila Trotman had four children and a fifth on the way. Fifteen full-time Navigators workers and a woman who helped Lila with the cooking, cleaning, and laundry that twenty-one people generated also lived in the house. Betty felt at home from the start, especially at dinner when everyone sat together around a huge oak table carrying on lots of lively conversation.

The day after Betty arrived, Dawson Trotman drove her to downtown Los Angeles where the Navigators had its main office. A space had already been cleared in the corner of the office for CAMF, and a desk, chair, and filing cabinet had been placed there for Betty to use. After thanking Dawson for the space, Betty set her leather satchel down on the desk. Inside it were several pages of notes that Jim Truxton had asked Betty to turn into a booklet on the aims of CAMF. After familiarizing herself with the new office, Betty took out a pencil and went straight to work. By the end of the day, she was pleased with what she had accomplished. Listed neatly on the page in front of her were eight aims for the new organization:

(1) To serve as a clearing house of information for airmen looking for ways to use their military training after the war.

(2) To provide missionary bases around the world where aircraft, pilots, and mechanics could be housed at the lowest possible cost.

(3) To help transport missionaries and their supplies to areas that were not accessible on commercial airlines.

(4) To help gather information on terrain and weather patterns in remote areas to make flying safer for missionaries.

(5) To supply traveling maintenance and repair units to serve all missionary aircraft around the world.

(6) To provide aircraft and pilots to help in emergency relief situations.

(7) To publish a newsletter keeping the public up-to-date on the work of CAMF.

(8) To establish CAMF groups in various countries that would help others to see and understand the importance of missionary work around the world.

As Betty reviewed the list, a feeling of satisfaction came over her. A broad smile spread across her face. She was pleased that God had directed her to be involved with others who had a vision similar to her own. She determined to do whatever was necessary to make the new organization successful.

A week later a typewriter arrived, a gift from Betty's father, who no longer needed it in his office. Betty put it straight to work as she typed up the eight aims into booklet form and wrote letters to people interested in the new organization.

As the days sped by, Betty came to appreciate Dawson Trotman. He was a networker, and he introduced her to many Christian men and women who would be key to the future of CAMF. He set up an appointment for her to meet Dr. Fuller, the voice behind the "Old-Fashioned Gospel Hour," a radio program that attracted ten million listeners, many of them in the military. Dr. Fuller was very impressed with the idea of an organization that would support missionaries with airplanes, and to show his support, he gave Betty a check for fifty dollars for CAMF.

The money came at just the right time to pay for the publishing of *Speed the Light on Wings of the Wind*, the name that had been given to the booklet containing the aims of CAMF. Thousands of copies of the booklet were produced and sent out to anyone who might be interested in the work of CAMF. As well, Betty set up a regular Tuesday night prayer meeting where people could gather to pray that God would bless the work of the new organization and direct the booklets into the right hands.

In December 1944, Betty was able to report to Jim Truxton, now stationed in Panama, that she was beginning to make a number of contacts as letters began to arrive in the mail in response to the booklet.

Christmas that year was Betty's second away from home. She spent it at the Trotman home with the other guests, where for some reason she was asked to play Santa for the gift exchange. She entered right into the spirit of the season, borrowing a large red bathrobe from one of the Navigators staff members and stuffing it with pillows. She put on a pair of red slippers, and Lila Trotman produced a Santa hat and whiskers from somewhere for her. Betty sprinkled flour on her hair to make it look white before putting on the hat and whiskers. Then she waited to make her entrance.

As she descended the sweeping staircase, with its mahogany paneling and chandelier sparkling overhead, she felt more like Scarlet O'Hara in *Gone with the Wind* than Santa Claus. As the last strains of "Jingle Bells" faded, Betty burst into the room yelling Merry Christmas. People erupted in laughter at the sight of her. She was, after all, known as one of the quieter, more reserved house guests. She reached into the pillowcase tossed over her shoulder and began pulling out presents.

A few days after Christmas there was more cause for celebration. The radio carried news that General MacArthur's forces, which had invaded the Philippines two months before, had finally forced the last of the Japanese to retreat. And in Europe, the German army's furious attack at the Battle of the Bulge had been turned back by determined American troops. The tide of the war was turning in the Allies' favor.

After Christmas Betty threw herself back into the work of CAMF. There was so much to do and only her to do it. She worked six days a week, often until seven at night, answering the ever increasing volume of people's inquiries about CAMF. To avoid writing the same thing over and over, Betty started a newsletter, which she called Missionary Aviation. Once again, Dawson Trotman proved helpful, suggesting she also send the newsletter to those on the Navigators mailing list to help get the news out about CAMF. Betty licked fifteen thousand stamps, and soon the newsletter was on its way to many different parts of the world. Within weeks, even more mail began pouring in, and Betty was in need of help to answer it all.

Betty was introduced to Selma Bauman, a Bible college student who volunteered to help her with some of the secretarial work. On her first afternoon at the office, Selma typed six letters to people who had inquired about CAMF. To her relief, Betty started to see the backlogged pile of correspondence begin to disappear.

As they worked, both Betty and Selma prayed regularly that God would clearly show the men they were writing to whether or not they should be involved in CAMF. One of the early responses was from an RAF flight instructor named Grady Parrott, an American stationed at Falcon Field in Phoenix, Arizona. The British government had hired Grady to help train young English pilots in the Royal Air Force Cadets. Grady's job was to train the pilots in advanced flight techniques and aerial combat maneuvers. Before the war, Grady had been an accountant, and Betty began to think of all the things an accountant would be useful for in a new ministry like CAMF. At every opportunity she prayed that God would direct Grady and his family to become involved with the organization.

In March 1945, Jim Truxton wrote to Betty from Panama that he would be stopping over in Los Angeles for two weeks on special assignment. Betty had told him about Grady Parrott, and Jim asked Betty to try to arrange a meeting between the two men. She got right on it, and when Jim Truxton arrived in Los Angeles, Grady Parrott was there to meet him. So, too, was Jim Buyers, who had served with him at Floyd Bennett Field in New York and was one of the original group of men who had conceived the idea of CAMF. Betty and the three men were soon talking like old friends. Although they came from differing backgrounds, they shared the same vision to use aviation to help spread the gospel. Together the four of them would become CAMF's first board of directors. CAMF was officially incorporated three months later. Jim Truxton was president, Grady Parrott vice president, Jim Buyers executive secretary, and Betty Greene secretary-treasurer. CAMF was now a fully licensed not-for-profit organization.

Despite having an official board of directors, most of the work still fell to Betty, who undertook the work cheerfully with Selma Bauman's help. In June, when the Navigators needed the office space back, CAMF moved to a small sixth-floor office in the Park Central Building overlooking Pershing Square. At about the same time, Jim Truxton's sister Margaret moved to Los Angeles, and she and Betty became friends. Soon Margaret was spending her days, and sometimes her evenings, with Betty and Selma answering mail from Christian airmen all over the world.

With the correspondence and office work now under control, Betty accepted more requests to speak about CAMF and its aims. She spoke at a conference in Los Angeles sponsored by the Church of the Open Door. Three thousand people sat quietly as Betty spoke about a new way to help missionaries to do their jobs safely and speedily using airplanes. After the talk, people flocked around Betty to ask how they could help the new organization. Betty jotted down the names and addresses of all those interested so they could be put on the mailing list to receive *Missionary Aviation*. The response was the same at most places Betty spoke.

But as busy as Betty was, one thing bothered her. It also bothered the three other members of the board of directors. Although they were sending out bags of newsletters by mail and answering many phone calls, CAMF did not have a single airplane or pilot actually out in the mission field. After all, that was the whole point of the organization.

The first glimmer of hope that the new organization might finally get to do what it was called to do came through Grady Parrott. Grady had a friend named Bill Nyman, who was on the board of Wycliffe Bible Translators (which also operated under the name Summer Institute of Linguistics, or SIL in some countries), an organization dedicated to writing down native languages that had previously never been recorded on paper and then translating the Bible into those languages.

Wycliffe Bible Translators had been invited by the Peruvian government to work with some of the remote Indian tribes in the Amazon jungle in the eastern part of the country. Although Wycliffe had experience in the jungles of southern Mexico, the Amazon basin was very different. Hundreds of miles of impenetrable jungle sometimes separated tribes, making it almost impossible to reach them overland. Wycliffe had decided it needed an air division, and Bill Nyman had approached Grady Parrott to be its first pilot.

Since Grady and his wife, Maurine, had already pledged themselves to work with CAMF, instead of going to work for Wycliffe, Grady spoke to Bill Nyman about CAMF's possibly supplying the airplanes and pilots needed to transport Bible translators and equipment into these remote areas. This prompted Wycliffe Bible Translators founder and director Cameron Townsend to ask CAMF to send someone to Mexico to meet with him and discuss the kind of air service it might be able to provide.

On September 2, 1945, World War II officially ended. Japan surrendered to American forces aboard the battleship *Missouri* anchored in Tokyo Bay. A week later, Betty Greene found herself on the first overseas mission for the Christian Airmen's Missionary Fellowship. She sat in a commercial airplane as it flew south through heavy thunderstorms. She was on her way to meet Cameron Townsend at a Wycliffe Bible Translators conference being held in Mexico City. She would be in Mexico for two weeks, and when she returned to Los Angeles, she would put together a report for the board of directors on how CAMF could help.

As she flew south, Betty wondered what lay ahead for her. She had read so much about missionary work and had studied foreign cultures for her degree. Now she was actually on her way to a foreign culture to meet real missionaries. She only hoped that a new, inexperienced organization like CAMF, with one full-time worker and no aircraft, could actually find a way to help a large, established ministry like Wycliffe Bible Translators.

Chapter 8

Mexico

The taxicab stopped in front of the Posada del Sol Hotel. Betty gasped when she saw the place. It was the most opulent hotel she had ever seen. For a moment she frowned, wondering how Wycliffe missionaries could possibly afford to meet in such a fine and expensive hotel as this.

The cab driver opened the door, and Betty followed him to the trunk to retrieve her two bags. Ten minutes later she was shown to a beautiful tiled room overlooking a small courtyard, complete with a trickling fountain. She unpacked her bags and put the book she was reading, *History of the Conquest of Mexico* by William Prescott, on the nightstand. She wanted to finish it while in Mexico to try to understand as much about the culture as possible.

Betty heard a knock at the door. When she answered it, there stood a vivacious young brunette. "Hello, I'm Marianna Slocum," the woman said, holding out her hand to shake Betty's. "I'm with Wycliffe Bible Translators in southern Mexico."

"Hello," Betty replied, shaking Marianna's hand. "I guess you already know I'm Betty Greene from CAMF."

Marianna nodded. "Uncle Cam told me to keep an eye out for you and bring you down to the conference room to meet the others. Are you ready, or do you need some time to freshen up?"

"I'm fine," Betty replied, eager to meet the missionaries.

As the two women walked together down the ornately carved staircase, Marianna Slocum explained that the hotel owner, Señor Galvant, a former governor of the state of Mexico, was a good friend of Cameron Townsend. Because of their close relationship, Señor Galvant was proud to offer Wycliffe Bible Translators hotel rooms at a fraction of their normal cost. Betty heaved a sigh of relief. She had been wondering whether she could actually work with an organization that would spend such large amounts of money on hotel rooms for its staff conferences.

Once she entered the meeting room, Betty was quickly introduced to about thirty people. (Betty was thankful that they were all wearing name tags.) Then she spotted "Uncle Cam," as Cameron Townsend was affectionately called, in the corner talking to a middle-aged couple.

"Over here, Betty," Cameron called when he saw her. "It's good to see you. I have some people I want you to meet. This is Bob and Lois Schnieder. They've offered to give you a tour of Mexico City when the conference is not in session. You'll be in good hands with them."

Betty smiled at the Schnieders.

"Is there anything in particular you'd like to see?" Bob Schnieder asked.

Betty's mind ran wild. "You'd be better asking if there's anything I don't want to see!"

They laughed together and started planning a trip to Chapultepec Castle, which Betty had read was built on the ruins of a gigantic Aztec temple.

The first two days of the conference passed quickly. While the Wycliffe missionaries met to discuss their common concerns about Bible translation and how to overcome them, Betty set about finding her way around Mexico City. She contacted a woman she knew from the WASP who was now vice president of Braniff Airlines and was visiting Mexico City at the time. Betty was particularly pleased when the woman arranged for her to fly a small plane at an airfield on the outskirts of the city. It was the first time she had flown in months, and she loved the freedom of once again soaring above the clouds.

On a visit to the federal aviation office to study Mexican aviation rules, Betty found that the rules were very similar to U.S. rules. She took a test on the spot and was given a pilot's license to fly in Mexico. It all happened so fast she could hardly believe it.

Between sessions at the Wycliffe staff conference, Betty talked with the missionaries. She asked them many questions about their aviation needs and jotted down pages of notes.

On Sunday she attended a Presbyterian Church with the Schnieders. While Betty herself was a Presbyterian, the service in Mexico was like nothing she had ever seen before. She sat wedged between an old Mexican man who constantly scratched his neck and a middle-aged woman with seven children neatly arranged to her left. To Betty, the church service was a mass of moving people. Old men constantly shuffled up and down the aisles, and women sitting near the open windows would yell to people outside. Without the crackling loudspeaker system that raised the pastor's voice above the crowd, Betty would not have been able to hear a word of the sermon, not that she understood it, since it was in Spanish.

The following day, the halfway point of the Wycliffe staff conference, Cameron Townsend asked Betty if she would consider extending her stay in Mexico and traveling down to Wycliffe's jungle camp where Bible translators did their final training before heading out to work in the field with a tribe or people group. The jungle camp, he assured Betty, would give her a taste of real missionary life and a chance to see the way airplanes could be used to help spread the gospel message.

Betty thought about it for several minutes. She had no pressing need to get back to Los Angeles.

Jim Truxton's sister Margaret and Selma Bauman were quite capable of running the CAMF office, and a lot could be gained from seeing missionary work firsthand. She agreed to Cameron Townsend's request. On October 12, 1945, Betty was one of a group of six people who boarded a narrow-gauge train bound for the city of Vera Cruz on the Gulf of Mexico. She sat beside Marianna Slocum as the train jostled them from side to side. Sometimes the carriage creaked so loudly Betty worried it might break apart, but somehow it held together, and the train chugged on through the day and into the night. To give herself some padding from the hard wooden slats of the seat, Betty curled up in the two blankets she had bought at an open market in Mexico City.

The night passed slowly. The train blew its whistle constantly and stopped often. At each stop, brown arms laden with items of food were thrust through the window at the group. "Compra esto, sólo dos pesos," they yelled, each trying to outdo the other. Betty was very hungry, and she waved two pesos in the direction of a young boy who was carrying an enormous bunch of thick bananas. The boy grinned, took the money, and handed three bananas to Betty, who sat back proudly and began to peel one. Howls of laughter filled the carriage. Betty wondered why everyone was looking at her, until she took a bite of her "banana." The fruit was hard and waxy!

"That's a cooking plantain," Marianna Slocum explained with a big grin on her face. "I've never seen anyone eat one raw."

Betty began to laugh. She had a lot to learn about living in another culture.

Finally the train arrived in Vera Cruz, and the six missionaries climbed out of their carriage. Since none of them had much money, they decided to spend the night sleeping on the dock instead of renting hotel rooms. That night Betty was introduced to coconut milk. She didn't like it much, but since coconuts were everywhere and were cheap, she forced herself to drink the liquid.

The next morning, feeling stiff and hungry, Betty climbed aboard another train, this time headed south toward the Pacific Ocean. Their destination was Juchitan, a short bus ride south of the train station at Ixtepec. They would spend a couple of days in Juchitan visiting two Wycliffe translators who had not been able to make it to the staff conference in Mexico City.

Marjorie MacMillan and Velma Packet stood at the side of the road waving as the dilapidated, overcrowded bus pulled to a halt to let the missionaries off. Betty was glad to get out and stretch her long legs.

Staying with the Bible translators was an eye-opening experience for Betty. Marjorie and Velma were in their early twenties and worked tirelessly to translate the Bible into Zapotecan, the local language. The group was scheduled to stay with them for only two nights, but Betty became ill with malaria, and it was a week before she felt well enough to travel again.

This time they headed east to Tuxtla Gutiérrez, the capital of Chiapas. Cameron Townsend had arranged for the new missionaries in the group to take a crash course in Spanish at a local high school there. Since Betty was with them, she took advantage of the opportunity to learn as much Spanish as possible. Who knew where her work with CAMF might take her—quite possibly someplace where Spanish would be useful.

While in Tuxtla, Betty visited the local airfield, where she met a man named Joe Urguidi. Although he was Mexican, Joe had learned to fly in St. Louis, Missouri, and was eager to speak with an American. He quickly offered to take Betty up for a spin in his 1927 model Travel Air.

Two weeks later, Betty was again in the cockpit with Joe Urguidi. This time she was on her way to El Real, a tiny airstrip three miles from Wycliffe's jungle training camp. With her were Cameron Townsend and an American businessman, Al Johnson, who was interested in the work of Wycliffe Bible Translators.

As the old Travel Air lumbered over steep mountains and across heavily forested valleys, Betty could see for herself the value of an airplane in such terrain. By the time they touched down at El Real airstrip, Betty and Cameron had decided an amphibious airplane would be the best choice for remote jungle flying, since it could land on the numerous rivers and lakes as well as on jungle airstrips.

As the airplane decelerated on the rough fifteen-hundred-foot-long airstrip at El Real, Joe Urguidi guided it to the right following the dogleg path of the runway. The reason for the dogleg was a small shed. Betty later found out the shed belonged to the airstrip owner Don Pepe, who used it to store chicle latex waiting to be flown to market. As the airplane rolled by the shed, Betty gave it a passing gaze. She had no inkling of the problems that shed would cause her and CAMF in the future.

Throughout the next two months living at the jungle camp, Betty had to keep reminding herself she was in a boot camp designed to prepare missionaries for remote and primitive situations. She shared a small mud hut with another woman, while another mud hut with a single stove in it served as camp kitchen. The schedule was every bit as demanding as her days in the WASP. She rose at 6 A.M., had breakfast at seven, and studied Spanish language from eight until ten. Then it was time for two hours of work in the garden, hacking away at the rocky ground in an attempt to grow vegetables to eat. Lunch was at twelve-thirty, followed by another hour of language study. The remainder of the afternoon until dinner was taken up with various other tasks. During this period, Betty studied maps and wrote a detailed report on the type of aircraft and support system that would be most suitable for Wycliffe Bible Translators work in Mexico and Peru.

Every day seemed to bring some new adjustment or challenge. Most had to do with the local animals. Rats scurried around the wooden beams in the kitchen, wild burros (donkeys) sneaked into the compound at night and ate the laundry from the clothesline, and a huge cow crashed through the kitchen door, knocking over everything. Mosquitoes hungrily swarmed around the missionaries wherever they went. Despite the hardships, Betty found it difficult to leave the group when Joe Urguidi flew his airplane in to pick her up on December 12, 1945. She'd had so many good times with the others and learned a lot in a short time.

Betty expected to be back in Los Angeles by December 18, but she had an unexpected delay along the way. When she got off her commercial airline flight in Mexico City, she felt almost too dizzy to stand up. Something was wrong! She collected her baggage and took a taxi straight to the nearest hospital. It turned out to be malaria again, only this time it was much worse than the bout she had experienced in Juchitan. Her doctor was puzzled by how sick she was, given the fact she had been taking quinine pills every day to ward off the disease. It was a medical mystery, but thankfully, once under the care of the hospital, Betty made a speedy recovery. On Christmas Eve she finally arrived back in Los Angeles.

The Trotmans welcomed Betty back for a second Christmas with them, and the Navigators staff at the house listened eagerly to her descriptions of Mexico and the work of Wycliffe Bible Translators there. Of course, the people she wanted to talk to most about her experiences were Jim Truxton, Jim

Buyers, and Grady Parrott, and as soon as Christmas was over, she would tell them about all that had happened. Nothing had been settled yet about CAMF and Wycliffe Bible Translators working together, but Betty was hopeful things would work out. CAMF needed a mission field to focus on so it could begin to turn its dreams into reality, and Wycliffe Bible Translators certainly needed some flying assistance.

In mid-January 1946, Betty opened a letter from Cameron Townsend. It was just what she had been hoping and praying for—an invitation from Wycliffe Bible Translators for CAMF to provide airplanes and pilots to meet the organization's flight requirements in Mexico and Peru.

Betty could hardly wait to phone the other CAMF board members and tell them the wonderful news. Now, if nothing else, they had a place to fly and a missionary organization that was prepared to give them a chance to prove themselves.

Chapter 9

No Better Man for the Job!

Three people sat at the table in the CAMF office. Betty was taking notes, Grady Parrott was sipping coffee, and Jim Truxton was speaking. "We have the green light from Wycliffe. All we need now is a pilot and a plane," he said.

Betty smiled to herself. It was true. With that single letter from Wycliffe Bible Translators, the work of CAMF had taken on a whole new urgency. The organization had a mission and needed to find a way to fulfill it.

"First, what pilot do we have that we could send to Mexico right now?" Jim asked.

Grady put down his coffee mug and cleared his throat. "As far as I can see, I'm out of the picture. There's still a lot of business planning to be done at this end, and I don't think I could ask anyone to take over that at short notice."

"Probably not," Jim agreed, running his hand through his wavy brown hair. "And Jim Buyers has left for Columbia Bible College to prepare for missionary work in Brazil. That leaves me and Betty."

Betty looked up from her note pad in surprise. She hadn't even considered the possibility that she could be CAMF's first pilot. "But, Jim, this was your vision first and foremost. I think you should be the one to go," she said.

Jim shook his head. "I've already got the next six months planned. There's so many churches I need to visit and so many returned servicemen I want to interview. This would be the wrong time for me to be away."

"How about that young man Nate Saint, the airplane mechanic? He has a pilot's license, too. He just didn't fly in the war because of some old leg injury," Grady interjected.

"I heard from him last week. He said he wanted to finish college before coming to join us," Betty said.

"Well, it looks as though you get to be CAMF's first pilot, Betty," Jim said with a smile. "I couldn't think of a better man for the job!"

Betty's head reeled as she thought about it.

"Now we need to get something for you to fly," Grady said. "I heard about a 1933 Waco biplane for sale. I think we should take a look at it."

Later that week, Betty and Grady checked out the Waco biplane. The aircraft was perfect for

CAMF. It had a 220-horsepower engine, a four-seater enclosed cabin, and a gleaming coat of new red paint on its wings and fuselage.

"How much do you want for it?" Grady asked the owner.

"I think she's worth five thousand dollars if she's worth a penny," the owner replied.

"We'll think about it," Grady said.

Betty and Grady walked quietly back to the car. Five thousand dollars was a lot of money. Once inside the car, the two of them paused a moment to pray and ask that if this was the airplane God wanted them to have He would show it by bringing in the money needed to purchase it.

Almost immediately money began to pour into the CAMF office. A church in Chicago familiar with the work of Wycliffe Bible Translators sent a check for fifteen hundred dollars to help with transporting Wycliffe missionaries. Wycliffe Bible Translators itself gave five hundred dollars, and a memorial fund set up to honor a Christian pilot shot down during the war provided another thousand dollars. Within a week, they had three thousand dollars toward the purchase of the plane. During his time in the military, Jim Truxton had managed to save two thousand dollars, and now he felt he should give the money to CAMF to make up the balance needed to buy the Waco biplane.

On February 23, 1946, a small crowd gathered by the airstrip at La Habra, California. Everything had fallen into place so quickly, and now it was time for Betty to set off on the twenty-one-hundred-mile flight to Mexico City and then on to the Wycliffe jungle camp in southern Mexico.

The sun beat down from a clear blue sky as Mr. Goodner, a Wycliffe Bible Translators board member, led the crowd in prayer. Then Betty climbed into the cockpit, ran through her preflight checklist, and cranked the Waco's engine to life. The engine purred smoothly as Betty taxied to the end of the runway. Betty turned the plane into the breeze and gunned the engine. Within moments, the Waco biplane was airborne. Betty circled the airstrip, dipping the plane's wings as she flew over the gathered crowd. After more than a year of planning and working in the office, she was finally doing what she'd dreamed of from that day seven years before when she had sought Mrs. Bowman's advice. Betty Greene had finally combined her love for God and missions with her love of flying.

The route Betty had mapped out for the trip took her east over Arizona and New Mexico and on into Texas before heading south into Mexico. The first night she landed in Phoenix, and the second in Marfa, Texas, southeast of El Paso. From there the Waco biplane eased its way along above the Rio Grande for a while and then turned south into Mexico. The plane made slow but steady progress, with Betty keeping its speed at a modest one hundred miles per hour.

At 8 A.M. on the fourth morning, Betty took off from Tuxpan, Mexico, headed for Mexico City. She had studied the relief maps carefully and knew she would have to circle the airfield several times while the Waco climbed to ten thousand feet to clear a mountain range east of Tuxpan.

The Waco biplane had just about reached altitude when Betty heard strange little popping noises. Frowning, she peered out the side window to see small pieces of something shooting from the back of the engine. She had no idea what it was and listened closely to the noise of the engine. It sounded fine. So she checked out the window again. Things where still coming from the engine. Could she have flown into a flock of birds? She didn't think so, but neither could she think of anything else to explain the problem. She had no option but to turn back. The last thing she needed was engine trouble crossing the razor-sharp mountain peaks that lay ahead.

Once back on the ground in Tuxpan, Betty went straight to work inspecting the engine. Unused to the sight of a woman with a wrench in hand working on an airplane, an airline worker came to help her. Two hours later, they determined that the problem was the Waco's shiny new red paint that Betty and Grady had so greatly admired. The paint on the engine cowling was flaking off, causing the noise and the trail of debris coming from the direction of the engine. By then it was too late to resume her flight. At about noon each day, an inversion layer developed over Mexico City, and Betty did not want to fly through it unless absolutely necessary. Much relieved that the problem was nothing serious,

Betty took to the sky again the following morning and this time had an uninterrupted flight into Mexico City.

The next day it was on to the Wycliffe jungle camp, though Betty had to adjust her flight plans a little because of poor weather conditions. Clouds hung low as she flew the airplane over the highest mountains she had yet encountered. The Waco biplane was constantly buffeted by updrafts and downdrafts. One downdraft pushed the plane down at a rate of two thousand feet per minute, demonstrating to Betty the need to have lots of extra altitude between the plane and the ground when flying over such mountainous terrain.

When Betty finally touched the Waco biplane down on the dogleg airstrip at El Real, a large group of Wycliffe workers was waiting to greet her and welcome her back. The workers were also glad to receive the mail and supplies she carried with her.

Betty was put to work the next day ferrying translators to Tapachula on the Guatemalan border. A Peruvian consul was there, and the translators all needed visas to enter Peru in April. As Betty ferried them on the one-hour-and-forty-five-minute flight, she looked down at the hills and jungle below, knowing that the same journey overland could take up to two weeks, and longer during the wet season. It made her feel good to be using an airplane to save missionaries hundreds of hours in travel time and prevent lots of discomfort.

Her first month based at the jungle camp sped by. Betty logged more than one hundred hours of flying. She single-handedly took care of the refueling and maintenance of the Waco, as well as the loading and unloading of it, while keeping a steady stream of letters flowing to CAMF headquarters to inform her partners about her progress. Toward the end of March, she was joined by CAMF's second pilot, George Wiggins, a solid, dark-haired ex-Navy flyer. George was to replace Betty in Mexico, freeing her to go on and help Wycliffe Bible Translators open up its new work in Peru. Betty was eager to get him acquainted with the Waco biplane and the intricacies of flying it in the Mexican jungle so that she could be on her way. She had no idea of the lesson in patience she was about to have.

George Wiggins flew with Betty on all the flights she made. Sometimes she was lead pilot, and other times he was. While they were in the air she went over all the lessons she'd learned about jungle flying, emphasizing the unexpected updrafts and downdrafts and the difference that humidity made in the distance it took to get a plane off the ground. She found George Wiggins to be a good learner and a careful and competent pilot. That's why she was never fully able to explain what happened on the morning of March 26, 1946.

Betty and George had spent the night in Tuxtla after flying a couple of Wycliffe missionaries there. The flight back to the El Real airstrip the following morning was uneventful, with George piloting the plane. As they approached El Real, Betty relaxed; George had turned out to be a good jungle pilot. His descent to the airstrip was a little fast and steep, but Betty wasn't worried; it was easily corrected. She felt the wheels of the Waco bump down onto the dirt and waited for George to brake. Nothing happened. The plane bounced along the airstrip and then thud! Betty whipped her head around to see what it was. The two left wings of the biplane had slammed into the shed in the crook of the dog-leg airstrip. Before Betty had time to react, the plane had spun 180 degrees and stopped in a cloud of red dust.

"Get out now!" Betty shouted, hardly able to process what had happened. "There'll be a fire!"

Betty heard George shut off the ignition, and the two of them scrambled out of the Waco biplane and ran for cover. They waited several minutes at the edge of the airstrip, but no fire broke out. They walked cautiously back to the airplane to examine the damage. The closer Betty got, the more her heart sank. The Waco was a mess. Both left wings had been snapped off like twigs, the propeller was twisted and broken, and the landing gear had collapsed, leaving the plane lying in a gouged-out pile of dirt.

Betty and George stood staring at the wreckage, too stunned to speak. CAMF's one and only airplane lay demolished in front of them. How was Betty going to tell Jim Truxton? What about all the money that had been donated for the plane? And what about all the people who had said flying missionaries around was just too dangerous? Were they right after all?

Later that day, a pilot flying overhead spotted the downed biplane and flew in to see whether anyone needed help. Betty took the opportunity to fly out to Tuxtla with him and then caught a commercial flight to Mexico City, where it took her two weeks to order new parts for the Waco and write an accident report. What she dreaded the most, however, was writing to Jim Truxton and the other members of the CAMF board to let them know what had happened. She knew how disappointed they would be.

In her mind, Betty went over and over the accident. She didn't know how George could have hit the shed. True, the radial engine of the Waco made it difficult to get a clear view from the front of the plane, but George had landed at the airstrip before and always avoided the shed. In the end she wrote, "Somehow it didn't seem to be a question of his handling of the ship, but an unexplainable failure to see the hut or remember it was there." The explanation did not satisfy Betty, but there was no other way to put it.

By mid-April, Betty had done all she could do in Mexico City and flew back to Tuxtla, where she stayed with a missionary family. While she waited there for news on parts for the Waco and for someone to come and repair it, she passed the time studying Spanish. The weeks dragged by with no definitive word from CAMF headquarters. They were having difficulty locating parts, and worse, no one had the necessary skills to repair the plane. Betty prayed hard and waited.

In June, the first parts for the airplane arrived along with news from the CAMF office in Los Angeles that a new staff member had been added to the team. His name was Charlie Mellis, a B-17 bomber pilot during World War II. Betty was glad for more staff, though it made her feel bad again about not having any aircraft. Another piece of information came from the office in Los Angeles: CAMF had changed its name to Missionary Aviation Fellowship (MAF) to align itself with another missionary aviation program sprouting in England.

Finally, in July 1946, Nate Saint, the pilot and airplane mechanic, arrived from Pennsylvania to repair the damaged Waco biplane. Although Nate had been planning to go to college, Jim Truxton had managed to recruit his services for the repairs. Betty flew to Mexico City to meet him. It was the start of the rainy season, and she was eager to fill him in on all the details and be on her way to her new assignment in Peru.

Knowing the Waco was in good hands with Nate Saint, Betty finally left Tuxtla for good three and a half months after the crash. Wycliffe Bible Translators had purchased a Grumman Duck, a 950-horsepower amphibious airplane, and was waiting for Betty to come and fly it in the Amazon jungle in the east of Peru where they were setting up linguistic and Bible translation bases.

As she studied the map of the Peruvian Oriente, as the vast jungle area east of the Andes Mountains was called, Betty wondered what adventures lay ahead for her. Once again, she was the only MAF pilot in the air, and she hoped for better luck with the Grumman Duck than she'd had with the Waco biplane.

Chapter 10

"Don't Fly Unless You Have To"

It was Thursday, July 11, 1946, and stepping off the Pan American Airlines flight in Lima, Peru, was one of the most memorable experiences in Betty's life. Waiting on the tarmac to greet her were Cameron Townsend, members of the British and American Bible Society, and Lieutenant Larry Montgomery of the U.S. Air Force. Cameron Townsend said a few words of welcome, and the lieutenant pinned a corsage on Betty's dress and presented her with the key to the Grumman Duck.

On the drive to the home of the Wycliffe missionaries Betty was to stay with, Cameron Townsend brought her up to date on things. The Grumman Duck, which had been christened *Amauta*, an Inca Indian word meaning "a wise man in service of his

101

people," had been officially handed over to Wycliffe Bible Translators three days before. Betty wished she could have been at the handing-over ceremony. It sounded like a wonderful affair. Representatives from both the American and the Peruvian governments had been present. This was because the United States Foreign Liquidation Commission had sold the Grumman Duck to Wycliffe very cheaply and the Peruvian government had agreed to pay half the purchase price and supply fuel to Wycliffe for only seventeen cents per gallon. The Peruvians had also agreed to pay half the cost for any repairs on the plane. For its part, Wycliffe had agreed to fly the airplane on missions for the Ministries of Education and Health. Cameron Townsend was pleased with the arrangement, not only because it would save Wycliffe Bible Translators money but also because of the goodwill and cooperation it would create with the government of Peru.

Later that same afternoon, after Betty had freshened up, the gates of the American Embassy in Lima swung open and Betty was escorted onto the grounds. She had been invited to have coffee with Ambassador Cooper, who promised he would do whatever he could to help Betty fulfill her mission in Peru.

The next morning, still excited by the welcome she had received, Betty took a cab to the airfield where the Grumman Duck was housed. She was eager to see the big plane and take it up for some test flights to learn its peculiarities. As she stepped from the cab, Betty was met by the steely gaze of Marine Corps General Ross Powell, head of the United States Navy Air Mission in Peru and under whose command the Grumman Duck had been used. She thrust out her hand to shake his, at the same time introducing herself. "Betty Greene, sir. I'm the one who's going to fly the Grumman Duck."

General Powell drew himself up to his full height and glared at Betty. He did not speak for a long moment. Then he said, "Huh! I wonder what Wycliffe thinks it's doing bringing a girl in to do a man's work!"

Betty felt herself turning red. She wondered how to respond to the general's remark. The last thing she wanted was to antagonize the chief American military officer in Peru. "I've been flying amphibians for six years," she said, thinking of the many times she had landed on Lake Washington. It seemed a long way away right at that moment.

"Have you ever flown over the Andes?" he asked, boring into her with his eyes.

"No, sir," Betty replied.

"Of course not!" the general bellowed. "No woman has ever flown over the Andes! Do you think you have what it takes to be the first? And have you navigated your way over the Amazon jungle?"

"No, sir," Betty replied again, biting her tongue to stop herself from saying more.

"She's a big ship, far too big for a woman to handle," General Powell continued, as if Betty hadn't yet been able to get his point.

"I have all the ratings required, and Wycliffe has designated me to fly the aircraft. They have complete confidence in me," she countered, and then added more forcefully, "I would appreciate your telling whoever it is who needs to know I am here so I can take the plane up for a test flight. I'm anxious to get started."

Although Betty was shaken by General Powell's attitude, she knew the worst thing would be to let him think he had upset her. Reluctantly, the general directed her to the hangar where the Grumman Duck was housed. He told her to ask for a Lieutenant White.

Lieutenant White was as kind and helpful as he could be under the circumstances. He gave Betty the manuals and sat in the cockpit with her explaining the airplane's special features. He was forbidden, however, by General Powell to take her up for a demonstration flight. As far as the Marines were concerned, Betty was on her own.

Surprised by the turn of events, Betty decided to make the best of the situation. She knew she could fly the amphibious biplane, and she told herself that no general was going to unnerve her. She sat in the front cockpit studying the manuals. After going through the checklist for engine ignition and takeoff, she cranked the plane to life. Soon the ungainly craft was lumbering down the runway and into the air. Betty circled above Lima, gaining altitude with each circuit.

Contrary to what General Powell had said, the Grumman Duck turned out to be one of the easiest airplanes she had flown. It performed well at twenty thousand feet, and with the throttle setting Betty had chosen, it used less than thirty-five gallons of fuel an hour. This was a lot less than the fifty gallons an hour the manual said it used. The engine, however, had a few knocks, and upon investigation, it was decided that the plane needed an engine overhaul. As a result, *Amauta* was not ready to fly until December.

It was December 20, 1946, five days before Christmas, when weather conditions finally looked promising enough for Betty to attempt to fly over the Andes mountain range and into the Oriente. She had begun the same flight three days before but had been forced back by foul weather. In the cockpit behind Betty was Cameron Townsend, not only because he wanted to be on the first flight over the Andes for Wycliffe Bible Translators' new airplane but also because he was going to operate the radio on the flight, since he spoke perfect Spanish.

By 9:15 A.M., *Amauta* was airborne and circling Lima to gain altitude before heading east over the Andes. As the plane circled, it was time for Betty to raise the landing gear. In most airplanes this procedure was a simple matter of turning a switch, but not so in a Grumman Duck. Betty had to manually turn a wheel in the cockpit to lift the eighteen-inch-diameter wheels up into their cavities. It was hard work, involving fifty-four turns of the wheel, with a final heave that took both of Betty's hands and all of her strength to achieve. Finally, Betty heard the clunk, and an indicator light blinked on in the cockpit, letting her know the wheels were safely retracted.

Thirty minutes after takeoff, the plane climbed ten thousand feet. It was now above Lima's almost constant blanket of cloud. Betty continued to guide the airplane up. When it reached sixteen thousand feet, she brought the nose of the plane around until it was pointed in an easterly direction. Although huge billowing clouds hung over the peaks of the Andes, Betty was confident she could find a way through the weather conditions this time. Below she spotted the trans-Andean highway, the highest highway in the world. From her maps she knew the best course across the Andes was to follow this highway at a safe altitude. As the plane flew along, every so often Betty would catch a glimpse of a mangled car or truck that had veered off the highway and plummeted to its destruction, sometimes thousands of feet below. The sight of these vehicles helped her focus on the job at hand!

The Grumman Duck pitched and rolled from updrafts as it crossed the western edge of the Andes Mountains. After that, the flying was smooth again as it flew across the seventy-mile-wide Andean plateau. Then, as suddenly as the mountains had begun, they fell away, and Betty could see the jungle far below in the distance. She looked back at Cameron Townsend. "Could you check if we are cleared to land at San Ramon?" she asked. "I don't want to begin descent until I know for sure."

Cameron nodded, clicked the switch on the side of the radio microphones, and began speaking in rapid Spanish.

"Cleared for landing," he called to Betty a minute or so later. "Bring her down."

Betty pushed the joystick forward, and the nose of the plane dropped. As the plane approached the military airfield at San Ramon, Betty turned the wheel fifty-four turns in the opposite direction to lower the landing gear. San Ramon lay at the junction of the Palca and Tumayo Rivers, and as the plane descended, Betty could make out sugar and coffee plantations nestled on the sides of the towering mountains.

It wasn't until the Grumman Duck was safely on the ground that Betty allowed herself a moment to celebrate. She had done it! She was the first woman to pilot an airplane across the Andes Mountains. But more exciting to her than that, she had flown an airplane into a remote spot where missionaries desperately needed its services.

The plan was to refuel the plane at San Ramon and then fly on to Pucallpa, two hundred miles to the north. However, the weather did not cooperate. Low clouds closed in around San Ramon, bringing with them rain. It was not until five days later, on Christmas Day 1946, that Betty was finally able to take off again.

Betty was able to use the Rio Pachitea as her guide, flying above it and following its course almost all the way to Pucallpa. As she was winding down the wheels for landing there, Betty spotted two people below.

"Joe and Jeanette Hocking," Cameron said, pointing in the direction of the couple. "We're in for a treat. Jeanette is the best cook this side of the Andes."

Cameron was right. Jeanette had a wonderful Christmas dinner of roast duck and vegetables waiting for them.

Over the next few days, Betty perfected taking off and landing on water, using a stretch of the river near Pucallpa. The biggest hazard was the partially submerged logs that could rip the bottom out of the airplane's floats in an instant, sinking the Grumman Duck. Betty tried her best to spot these hazards, and she prayed hard, too! Once everything checked out with landing and taking off on water, there was plenty of work for Betty and *Amauta* to do. Wycliffe missionaries needed to be ferried to and from the new camps that were being created in the Amazon jungle. By the end of January, Betty had completed twenty-three flights over the jungle.

At the end of January, Betty returned to Lima, where a large celebration was held to honor the Peruvian Air Force and the role it was playing in helping Wycliffe. At the celebration, Betty was presented with a pin commemorating her as the first woman to pilot a plane across the Andes. Betty felt a strange sense of justice in receiving the honor, given the doubts General Powell had expressed about her ability to fly the Grumman Duck.

After several days in Lima, it was back to the jungle to transport more Wycliffe missionaries. Betty had been doing this for several months when Larry Montgomery, the lieutenant who had greeted her on her arrival in Lima, came to join her as second pilot and aircraft mechanic. Larry had been discharged from the military and had joined MAF. Naturally, Betty was delighted to have him. It relieved her of some of her flying duties, and there was now someone to regularly service and maintain the airplane.

During their times flying the Grumman Duck, they both noticed a slight vibration in the engine. While they were staying in the town of Iquitos, Larry decided to do some engine maintenance. In the midst of the work, he received an urgent message that his family needed him in Lima as soon as possible. He booked a flight to Lima on a commercial airliner and reported to Betty on the state of the engine. His last words echoed in her mind as she dropped him off at the airport: "Don't fly unless you have to."

While Betty would have liked to have had the aircraft at her disposal, she understood Larry's need to leave. Besides, he would be back in a few days, and most likely there would be no need for any emergency flights while he was gone. However, that was not to be. On June 15, 1947, the commandant of Itaya Military Base contacted Betty. "The situation does not look good," he said. "Two of my men took off in a plane several hours ago for a short flight. They have not returned and would have run out of fuel by now. I'm sure they must have gone down somewhere over the jungle."

"Was it a float plane?" Betty asked hopefully, thinking that if it was, they might have been able to land on one of the rivers.

"No, it was not," he replied grimly.

Betty's mind raced. What should she do? Larry Montgomery had told her to fly only if she had to. Was this an emergency worth the risk of flying the Grumman Duck? When she thought about the men possibly lying injured in the twisted wreckage of a crashed airplane, she knew she had to take the risk and try to find them. The commandant was grateful.

As soon as the airplane was fueled, Betty began flying low over the rivers near the military base. In the vast green carpet of the Amazon jungle, most pilots used the rivers as points of reference to navigate from. After five hours of flying, the shadows across the jungle were lengthening, and Betty knew it was time to head back for the night. Although she had not located the crashed plane or the two men, at least the Grumman Duck's engine had run perfectly.

The following morning, Betty took to the skies again, this time with the commandant in the cockpit behind her acting as a spotter. Another man, Francisco, rode in the plane's hold. They searched for three hours along the Rio Napo. With each passing hour, their hopes of finding the downed airplane dimmed. Finally, the commandant suggested they return to Iquitos to reassess the situation. Betty heaved a sigh of relief. While the Grumman Duck was performing flawlessly, she couldn't get Larry Montgomery's last words to her out of her mind. She climbed to two thousand feet and began the return trip, following the Rio Napo as she did so, hoping her two passengers would catch a glimpse of something below.

Betty noted the approaching bend in the Rio Napo. This meant they were nearing the town of Oro Blanco and were right on course for the return flight. Then suddenly there was silence. Total silence. The plane's engine had quit. Betty heard the commandant gasp behind her. She knew she had to remain calm; their lives depended on it. She tried to start the engine again. Nothing happened, and they were losing altitude fast. In less than a minute they would hit the ground. Betty scanned the scene in front of her. The bend in the river made the stretch of water where she estimated they would come down too short to land on. She said a quick prayer under her breath and tried the engine one last time. The engine sputtered to life, and Betty pulled back on the joystick to gain more altitude. The heavy plane climbed about twenty feet before the engine fell silent again. However, with the few moments of power it had given, Betty realized she now had enough altitude to glide the plane past the bend in the river to a stretch of water she could put the plane down on. She quickly made the course adjustment and prepared for an emergency landing.

Bang! The Grumman Duck's floats hit the water, and the plane was dragged to a quick stop. Within a minute of flying at two thousand feet in the air, it was floating on the waters of Rio Napo.

The commandant clambered out of the rear cockpit and onto the lower left wing. His face was white with shock. "Señorita," he called to Betty, "how can you be so calm at a time like this?"

"God was with us," Betty replied. "He has brought us safely to the ground."

The commandant nodded as the color began to return to his face. "It is as you say!" he said.

Betty had just begun to ponder how to get the powerless airplane to the side of the river when a canoe paddled by two Indian men emerged from the jungle overhang at the edge of the river. The men smiled and waved cheerfully, and when they spotted Francisco, they called him by name.

"There's a rope in the hold," Betty yelled to Francisco. "Tie one end to the cleat on the front of the right float and give the other end to the men. Ask them to drag us ashore."

Francisco nodded, and soon *Amauta* had been towed to the water's edge, where she was tied to a huge ironwood tree.

The commandant was unable to contact anyone back at base on the radio. The three of them settled down to eat their emergency rations and spend a restless night in the airplane, hoping the atmospheric conditions in the morning would allow them to get a radio transmission through to base. That is exactly what happened, and a Faucett floatplane was dispatched to collect them. Several military men were left to float the Grumman Duck back along the rivers to Iquitos.

By the time the plane finally arrived back at Iquitos, Larry Montgomery had returned and was waiting to see what had gone wrong. He made a quick check of the engine and found the main pinion gear had been broken. As he examined the engine, he could not figure out how Betty had managed to get it started again to give her the few seconds of power she needed to make a safe landing.

The damage to the engine was irreparable. A replacement engine would need to be fitted to the plane, and the nearest one was located in Panama. It would take about two months to ship it to Peru from there.

Betty expected to fly the airplane again as soon as it was fitted with its new engine, but it wasn't to be. Her flight over the Rio Napo was the last flight she ever took in the Grumman Duck. A week after the engine failure, she received a letter from home. Her father was not well, and her mother was having a difficult time coping. Betty felt she should go home and help her mother out for a while.

Betty was sure that Larry Montgomery would be able to carry on the work she had begun. Besides, the vision of MAF and Wycliffe Bible Translators was changing. Wycliffe had decided it needed airplanes that would service only its many outposts as well as meet any obligations it had to the Peruvian government. At the same time, MAF had made a commitment to serve missionaries from any denomination or group who were working in a particular area. In the meantime, Cameron Townsend decided to start JAARS (Jungle Aviation And Radio Service), a fully fledged branch of Wycliffe Bible Translators. He had invited Betty to help found this new organization. As flattered as she was by the invitation, she declined. Her heart was with MAF and its vision of serving all missionaries and mission organizations around the world. Betty returned to Los Angeles for a debriefing with MAF and then traveled to Seattle to check on her parents.

Chapter 11

A New Assignment

It was not until she was back home in Evergreen Point that Betty realized just how exhausting the previous two years of pioneering missionary aviation had been. So while she kept in close communication with Missionary Aviation Fellowship and continued to serve on its board of directors, she felt she needed a change of pace.

In the fall of 1948, Betty enrolled in a master's degree program at the University of Washington. She majored in Latin American studies, having developed a strong interest in Latin culture during her time in Mexico and Peru.

During vacations she traveled to Los Angeles to work in the MAF office. She also ferried two MAF airplanes to Mexico, one in January and another in

July 1950. Wherever she went, Betty was an enthusiastic ambassador for MAF, speaking about the opportunities for service that existed within the organization.

During this time, Betty also made friends with David and Annette Weyerhaeuser, who owned a huge lumber company in the Northwest. It was through their friendship with Betty that the Weyerhaeusers decided to donate their Stinson Voyager aircraft to MAF for use in Ecuador. Betty was even more pleased about the donation when she learned that Nate Saint would be the one flying it. Nate was the person who had single-handedly rebuilt the crashed Waco biplane in Mexico. He and his wife, Marj, were now heading up MAF's new work in the Ecuadorian Oriente. From her work in Peru, Betty knew just how much help a light single-engine plane like the Stinson would be.

In December 1950, Grady Parrott asked Betty to consider relieving pilot Clarence "Soddy" Soderberg, who for the past four years had been flying for the Sudan Interior Mission (SIM) on loan from MAF. The work in Nigeria had grown to a point where Soddy's airplane was not enough, and a second pilot, John Clay, and a second airplane had joined Soddy there. Now Soddy and his wife, Alice, were due to return to the United States for a two-year furlough. Betty eagerly accepted the opportunity to get back into active flying service with MAF.

On February 18, 1951, Betty found herself sitting on a commercial airliner on the final leg of her nine-thousand-mile journey from Seattle to Kano, in northern Nigeria. Her excitement grew as the airplane winged its way south over the countries of Algeria and Niger.

Finally, at 2 A.M., Betty stepped off the plane into the warm, humid air of Kano. She could make out Soddy Soderberg waving at her from behind a wire fence at the edge of the tarmac. She waved back enthusiastically. She had made it! She was once again an active missionary with Missionary Aviation Fellowship.

As Soddy's car sped west through the old city, Betty peered up at the clear, starry night sky. There was the Southern Cross. She hadn't seen it since leaving Peru.

Before long, Soddy announced they were entering the SIM compound. Betty was impressed as he pointed out the eye hospital, health clinic, print shop, church, and guest houses. But Soddy saved the best for last. Swinging the car left, he pointed out the aluminum hangar that gleamed in the moonlight. Parked safely inside were MAF's two airplanes stationed in Nigeria.

The first thing Betty needed to do was to get a Nigerian pilot's license. The next day, Soddy flew her south to Nigeria's capital city Lagos on the coast of the Gulf of Guinea. Everything went without a hitch, and on the return flight, Soddy suggested they fly into the SIM center at Jos. This was a huge complex with a large hospital and guest houses. Compared to the runways in Peru, those in Kano and Jos were a dream to land on. They had no high mountains or tall jungle trees around them, and no stray animals had wandered onto them. They were just long, hard, well-defined stretches of dirt.

A week later, Betty said farewell to the Soderbergs as they left to take their furlough and threw herself into the work of flying for SIM in Nigeria. There was always something that needed to be done—medical teams to be flown into remote areas, the children of missionaries to be ferried to and from boarding school, and sick people to be transported to the hospital.

Betty enjoyed the challenge of flying in Nigeria, especially over the southern reaches of the Sahara Desert that spilled into the north of the country. Here, where there were few landmarks, it was easy to become disoriented and lost. In fact, only two years before, the pilot flying an Italian airliner on a scheduled flight from Rome to Kano had become lost. Disoriented, he finally landed the plane in the desert a thousand miles west of his destination. The pilot was killed in the ensuing crash, but the passengers were rescued by a passing camel train. Betty soon learned that as in the jungle, the best way to scout out a new route was to follow something on the ground, such as a riverbed, a road, or even a camel track.

It was not long before Betty had learned about one of the more interesting weather features of northern Nigeria—the harmattan. The harmattan occurred when winds blew from the north in the dry season. With it came thousands of tons of sand from the Sahara, whipped up and driven south in enormous sandstorms. It was very difficult to fly through these ferocious storms, since the wind-driven sand made it nearly impossible to see a foot in front of the airplane.

Betty experienced her first harmattan in May while in Sokoto, 230 miles west of Kano. She had flown to Sokoto to collect an expectant mother and take her to the hospital at Jos to give birth. She landed in Sokoto, and although she wanted to leave her Cessna airplane parked in a hangar overnight, the airport attendant insisted she leave it in the open. He assured her he would tie the plane down extra tightly using extra weights. Reluctantly, Betty agreed.

After a meal at the Johnses' home, where she was staying for the night, Betty looked out the window and noticed the wind was picking up. The palm trees in the yard were flapping about, and Betty began to wonder whether the Cessna was okay. She was thankful that the Johnses understood her concern and offered to drive her to the airport to check on the plane. However, the offer proved harder to carry out than expected. The wind continued to steadily pick up, and Mr. Johns had to stop the Chevy pickup several times and get out to check that it was still on the road. It took two hours to reach the airport, and by the time they arrived a howling harmattan was blowing.

Mr. Johns pulled the pickup to a halt near the Cessna. The scene made Betty's heart pound. The Cessna was still there, but with every gust of wind its wheels lifted off the ground and then thumped back down again.

"Come on," Betty yelled to Mr. Johns over the howl of the wind. "We have to lift the back of the plane up, or it's going to take off without me!"

"I'll stay here and pray," Mrs. Johns said.

"We'll need all the prayers we can get," Betty replied. "See those six weights tied to the wings and tail? They weigh a hundred pounds apiece, and they're bobbing around like they were made of cork!" She pulled the collar of her jacket tight around her neck. "Are you ready?" she called to Mr. Johns as she opened the door of the pickup and climbed out.

The wind-blown grains of sand felt like needles as they pelted against Betty's exposed face and hands. Betty and Mr. Johns dashed toward the airplane.

"We have to wedge the tail of the plane up. There's too much lift on the wings when the wind blows the way she's sitting. We have to change the aerodynamics on the wing," Betty yelled against the wind.

Betty quickly looked around for something that would do the job. A pile of concrete anchor weights sat by the side of a nearby building. "Over there," Betty called, pointing in their direction.

Betty and Mr. Johns worked together to pull two of the one-hundred-pound blocks from the pile over to the Cessna. At one point, Betty's legs collapsed under the enormous weight she was dragging, but the sight of her airplane flailing about in the wind got her up and moving again.

Twenty minutes later, the pair had managed to prop up the tail of the Cessna with the weights.

Sure enough, this changed the flow of air over the wings, and the aircraft no longer bounced into the air with each gust of wind. Instead it stayed sitting firmly on the ground. Satisfied with their effort, Betty gave Mr. Johns the thumbs-up, and the two of them dashed back to the pickup. They all sat in the pickup for an hour until the wind died down enough for Betty and Mr. Johns to push the Cessna into the hangar, where Betty had wanted to park the plane in the first place.

Every muscle in her body ached as Betty lay in bed that night, and her skin stung from the sand-blasting it had received. Still, knowing her plane was safe, she slept soundly. The next morning, Betty flew the expectant mother to the hospital at Jos, where the woman gave birth to a baby boy the following day.

About three months after her experience with the harmattan, Betty experienced another world—that of the sultan. She was flying Dr. Helser, SIM's director of leprosy medicine, and two of his staff to Sokoto to discuss the doctor's work with the sultan there. As they flew, Betty asked Dr. Helser all sorts of questions about the sultan. She was fascinated by the answers Dr. Helser gave. The sultan, a man in his mid-thirties, was the great grandson of Usman dan Fodio, a legendary Islamic teacher and writer on Sufi doctrine. In fact, Usman dan Fodio's body was buried in the grounds of the palace where the present sultan lived. By the time Betty had brought the Cessna to a halt at the airport in Sokoto, Dr. Helser had come up with an idea.

"Betty, you sound as though you're very interested in the sultan. Would you like me to see if I could get you clearance to come with me and my two aides?"

Betty's heart leapt with excitement. "That would be very kind of you," she said, trying to keep her hopes under control. After all, sometimes there was miles of red tape to go through to get even the most simple of things done in Nigeria.

Dr. Helser talked to the guards at the palace, and amazingly, within ten minutes it was all arranged. Betty would finally get to see a real sultan.

Betty, Dr. Helser, and his two aides were ushered into a long, dark corridor, lighted only by oil lamps hung high on the solid stone walls. With each step, Betty felt as if she were going back to medieval times. Suddenly, the guard leading them stopped abruptly.

"You must remove your shoes and proceed in bare feet," he said in very correct English.

Betty slipped off her shoes and put them neatly against the wall.

"Come, now, it is time to enter," the guard said.

Dr. Helser and his two aides walked ahead of Betty as they made their way through gilded doors and into an immense, darkened room. Betty squinted as her eyes adjusted to the low level of light. She followed the others, her feet scarcely making a sound on the plush Persian rug.

Soon they stopped in front of a platform. On the platform, a man dressed in white sat on a throne draped with a beautiful leopard skin. Dr. Helser bowed to the man, and Betty followed his lead.

"Ah, I see the doctor of lepers has come back to see me!" the sultan exclaimed with genuine pleasure in his voice. "And who is it you bring with you?"

Dr. Helser introduced the group and told the sultan all about the work Betty was doing in the region. The sultan was surprised but pleased to see a woman pilot, and he questioned Betty about the plane and her flying experience.

The doctor talked to the sultan about his work treating leprosy, and everything went well. When it was time to leave, the sultan even got off his throne and walked the missionaries back through the corridor to the entrance of the palace.

"So are you flying out right now?" the sultan asked.

"Yes," Betty replied. "We're hoping to get back to Kano before dark."

Dr. Helser joined in. "We will fly over the palace for Your Majesty, if you would like," he offered.

"I would like that a great deal," the sultan said.

As the Cessna gained altitude, Betty steered it east over the palace. She dipped its wings and looked out the side window. She could see the sultan waving enthusiastically below.

A month later, Betty found herself in another palace. This time she was accompanying her friend Helen Dixon. Helen ran the SIM guest house in Kano and had been teaching the wives and concubines of Kano's emir how to sew. When Betty told her how fascinated she had been to meet the sultan, Helen invited Betty to go along on her next scheduled sewing lesson at the emir's palace.

As Helen parked the car and walked across the courtyard toward the palace, she explained to Betty that although she taught the women to sew, she would much rather teach them to read. This was impossible, however. Females in the emir's palace were forbidden to learn to read for fear they might read something that would corrupt them. Sewing and embroidery were considered safe skills for women to learn.

Just as at the sultan's palace in Sokoto, there were many guards at the emir's palace. They all recognized Helen Dixon, and soon she and Betty were safely inside. Helen led the way through a series of twisting corridors deep into the palace until they came to a heavily guarded door. The guards nodded at Helen and opened the wooden doors that led into a large, richly decorated room. In the center of the room stood an enormous mahogany canopy bed overlaid in gold and mother-of-pearl. Betty had never before seen such a beautiful piece of furniture.

A tall woman stepped from the shadows and warmly welcomed Helen. Several velvet-covered couches lined the walls of the room, and the woman, obviously one of the emir's wives, invited Helen and Betty to sit. Soon they were surrounded by three of the emir's four wives and about half a dozen of his concubines. The women were all eager to show Helen the progress they had made with their sewing, but they were even more eager to hear any news of the outside world that Helen might be able to tell them.

Helen introduced Betty and told the women she was a pilot. For a moment there was stunned silence, and then the women started up with a rabble of questions. "Surely you mean you have only sat in an airplane?" "Helen is not saying a woman could drive an airplane as a man drives a car, is she?" "Aren't you afraid to be up so high?" "Do you take a man with you in case something goes wrong and you need help?" "What does your husband say about this?" "Does your father allow it also?"

Betty smiled at the questions and answered each one. She understood the sheltered lives these women lived. Helen had told her that apart from two holy days, when the women were allowed to go and peer out through the portals in the outer courtyard, they never left the suite of rooms they were now in. They did not see the sun. They did not go to the market—or anywhere else in the wonderful city of Kano.

As Helen drove Betty back to her house, Betty was grateful that she had so much freedom. She was free to read, free to have her own opinions, free to have her own faith, and free to soar above the clouds. She never again flew over the emir's palace without praying for the women confined within its walls.

Chapter 12

It's Not Harmattan

Betty sat in the cockpit of her trusty Cessna. Today she was going to ferry a missionary, Mrs. Ruten, and her newborn baby back home to Diapaga, Upper Volta (now called Burkina Faso). She had laid out a meticulous flight plan. From Kano she would fly westward to Sokoto, stop there for refueling, and then head in a northwesterly direction to Niamey, Niger, where she would again refuel. From Niamey she would head southwest to Diapaga.

As always, Betty had arrived at the airport an hour before she was due to depart so that she could check out the plane and supervise refueling. As she strolled across the tarmac to the hangar, she noted that it was going to be another bright, sunny day. Not a cloud was in the sky.

Everything went according to plan, and by 6:45 A.M., Mrs. Ruten was buckled snugly in the back seat with her new baby son nestled in a woven basket beside her. Betty cranked the plane's engine to life and taxied onto the runway. She set the throttle to full, and the Cessna sped off down the runway, pulling itself into the air as the early morning sun glistened on its wings. Betty guided it up to five hundred feet before banking right until the aircraft pointed west.

As they flew back over the airport, Betty could see the emir's official below standing between two splendidly decorated camels. The official raised a long horn to his lips and blew. Although she could not hear the sound over the noise of the engine, Betty smiled and waved. To her, some things about life in Kano seemed as though they were taken right from the pages of *The Arabian Nights*. The emir's official with his horn was one of them. Every day he stood at the entrance to the airport ready to salute with his horn any incoming or outgoing flights. Betty had no idea, though, why he always had two camels with him, other than that it added a dramatic touch to the scene.

Flying over the desert took extra care, since there were few landmarks to guide them. Betty asked Mrs. Ruten to help her look out for a particular town as they flew on in the morning air. Finally, the town of Kauro Namoda came into view. It was located on the bend of a dry riverbed, and Betty heaved a sigh of relief when she saw it. With the town beneath her, she knew she was on course and about two-thirds of the way to Sokoto.

Traveling on they spotted a caravan of camels below them. Betty dipped her left wing and banked around for a closer look at the fascinating sight.

"They're probably headed for Kano," Betty said to Mrs. Ruten, who stared down at the sight. "I met a group of them in Kano once when I was shopping with Ray de la Haye. They belong to the Tuareg people, and Ray talked to them in Tamashek. It turns out they travel hundreds of miles in caravans like that to trade dates for corn and cloth."

"I guess dates are what's in those bulging bags on the camels," Mrs. Ruten replied.

Betty nodded. "They were some of the fiercest men I've ever seen," she said. "They had huge curved swords and two or three daggers each with them, but they were very friendly to Ray and me."

As Betty guided the Cessna toward their refueling stop, she and Mrs. Ruten passed the time talking.

"It was too bad about what happened to the chief of the airport," Mrs. Ruten said. "I think a person is much safer flying over the Sahara than driving through it."

Betty nodded again. She had heard about the fate of the Englishman who had managed the airport in Kano until just before she had arrived in Nigeria. The Englishman had retired and, wanting an adventure, decided to travel overland from Kano to the Mediterranean coast rather than take a commercial flight. Apparently the trip had been well-planned. The man took several others with him, and they followed an ancient route used by slave traders for eight or ten centuries. The route had been well marked with fifty-five-gallon oil drums, but somehow something went wrong. A month after leaving Kano in high spirits in their three Landrovers, the remainder of the party straggled back to Kano dazed, exhausted, and dangerously dehydrated. The retired airport manager was not with them. He had died along the way and was buried somewhere out in the desert. No one ever quite knew what went wrong on the trip, other than that they had encountered a harmattan, lost their way, and run out of water. As Betty looked down at the vast expanse of sand, she could appreciate just how easily someone traveling across the desert could get lost, even if he had taken precautions.

Soon the monotonous hum of the engine put Mrs. Ruten and her baby to sleep, and Betty was the only one awake as the city of Sokoto appeared on the horizon. Far to the north of the city she could see haze rising into the morning air, and she wondered what it could be. She made a mental note to mention it to the air traffic officer on the ground.

As the Cessna landed, Betty's two passengers awoke. Mrs. Ruten was grateful to be able to climb out of the airplane for a while. Betty suggested she find the passenger waiting area and wait there until the refueling was complete. By now the day had turned very hot, and even though it had no air conditioning, the waiting area was shady and cooler.

Betty stood by the plane as six barefooted African men dressed in military khaki rolled out a fifty-five-gallon drum of fuel. A handpump was attached to the top of the drum. Once the cap was removed from the Cessna's fuel tank in the wing with a flourish, one of the men produced a piece of chamois. The cloth was used to strain the fuel as it was pumped by hand into the plane's fuel tank. When they had finished, Betty thanked the men and screwed the fuel cap back in place.

As Betty walked around the airplane checking to be sure everything was in order, another African man walked up to her. In his hand were some papers. Betty guessed that it was the latest weather information.

"Good morning," he said. "I see you have a clear day for your travels. Where are you flying to from here?"

"I'm on my way to Niamey, and then Diapaga."

"Very good. Here is the weather chart. It's a good day to be flying."

Betty laid the chart down on the hot tarmac and crouched to study it. She could see nothing on the chart to explain the haze she'd spotted on the horizon as she flew in. She decided to ask about it. "When I was flying in I thought I saw a haze to the north. Could it possibly be harmattan?" she asked.

The African knitted his eyebrows together and shook his head vigorously. "No! No way at all. It's too late for harmattan." He drew himself up to his full height and then added, "I can assure you most definitely, you will not be headed into harmattan."

"I wonder what the haze was then?" Betty questioned, hoping not to insult the African by questioning his report.

The African shrugged his shoulders. "It cannot be more than a swirl of sand. It is nothing to worry about," he assured.

Betty thanked him and, after studying the weather chart a little longer, went to find her passengers and get ready for takeoff on the second leg of the journey.

Once they were airborne, Betty double-checked the map for the points on the ground she would be looking for during the flight to make sure she was on course—a road that ran south to north, a small village, and a rocky outcrop. They weren't much to go on, but if the weather was as good as she'd been assured it would be, Betty felt the points would be enough to guide her to Niamey.

They had been flying for about twenty minutes when Betty started to get concerned. The haze she had seen in the distance was getting closer, and instead of being a thin cloud of dust, it looked more like a solid wall of sand. Ten minutes ticked by. Betty checked her compass. She was still on course, but sand was whipping around the Cessna, and visibility was dropping fast. Betty wondered about turning back, but she decided to keep pushing on as long as she could see five miles ahead. She didn't think it could be harmattan. After all, she had been assured by someone familiar with the local weather conditions that it was not harmattan season. It could only be a localized sand squall, and she reassured herself she would be through it in a few minutes.

After forty minutes in the air, Betty knew it was no localized sand squall. She was flying in a harmattan. She scanned the ground for the Niger River. Spotting it would relieve some of her anxiety. She could follow the river northwest to Niamey. An hour into the flight, visibility dropped to three miles. It was the halfway point in the flight, and Betty agonized over whether to turn back or keep heading for Niamey. While a small airplane like a Cessna, without a radio beacon, could take days to locate if it was downed in the Sahara, Betty felt she should keep going, as long as the visibility got no worse.

Much to her relief, conditions began to improve, and Betty was congratulating herself for making the right decision when sand began pelting her windshield again and visibility plummeted. She stayed calm. The worst thing a pilot could do in such a situation was panic. Despite her calm demeanor, she was genuinely concerned about their situation. Her mind was spinning as she tried to decide the best thing to do. Finally she decided to make a rapid descent in hopes of finding a suitable landing place on the ground. She pushed the yoke forward, and the nose of the Cessna dropped. The plane dropped from sixty-five hundred feet to twenty-five hundred before Betty could see the ground. Alas, it was all dunes. Betty had nowhere to land, so she decided to turn south in hopes of finding the road to Niamey (indicated on her map). By now it was too late to turn back, and the road was their best hope.

Betty's eyes scanned the ground beneath her as she looked for anything that could possibly be a road. She flew over a dry swamp, but it was not marked on the map, and she couldn't use it to help fix her position. Then, from amid the golden swirl of sand, she saw what she was looking for: a single-lane, red clay road. She brought the plane down farther to keep the road in view as she began to follow it toward Niamey. She had never before flown skimming along so close to the ground, except when she was landing. The only time she dared take her eyes off the ground below was to check her altimeter.

The ribbon of road below was their lifeline, and the minutes ticked by slowly as Betty flew above it, guiding the Cessna northward. Eventually the road widened, and Betty saw signs of civilization. She breathed a prayer of thanks as she pulled the plane up to ten thousand feet and spotted Niamey airport.

Betty radioed for permission to land and then guided the Cessna down the runway for a landing. As she taxied across the tarmac, relief surged through her. It was the closest she had come to a catastrophe since the engine of the Grumman Duck had failed in flight in Peru and she'd been forced to make an emergency landing on the river.

The propeller came to a halt. As Betty helped Mrs. Ruten and her baby out from the backseat of the plane, she said, "We'd better see if we can find somewhere to stay for the night. I'm not flying a foot farther in this weather."

The two women battled the wind and sand as they made their way to the main airport building. With the wooden doors finally shut behind them, Betty stopped a moment to enjoy the silence. She hadn't realized how noisy the harmattan was.

A French officer greeted Betty with a tip of his hat. "Welcome to Niamey, Mademoiselle. I am surprised to see you here on a day like today."

"Yes," Betty replied grimly. "The weather is very poor. I would have stayed on the ground in Sokoto if I had known."

"I have never seen the weather so poor this time of year," the French officer said, shaking his head. "A harmattan in this season, it is unheard of."

Twenty minutes later the Cessna had been secured for the night, and some local missionaries were on their way to pick up Betty, Mrs. Ruten, and her baby to house them for the night.

A young man who introduced himself as Don grinned from behind the wheel of an old Model A Ford sedan. "Come on in," he said. "Let's get you in out of this storm."

As Betty climbed in she marveled at the near perfect condition of the old car. On the drive to the mission station, Don told her the secret to the car's rust-free condition was the hot, dry air of the Sahara.

At the mission station a bowl of hot soup and a loaf of fresh baked bread awaited them. After dinner Betty, exhausted from the flight, excused herself and headed for the guest bedroom.

All night and through the next day the harmattan roared. It was not until the following day that the weather cleared and Betty felt confident to continue on with the last leg of the flight.

This time the trip went without a hitch, and four hours after takeoff from Niamey, Betty spotted the town of Diapaga. As they flew low over a group of houses, Mrs. Ruten pointed out her home, a single-story structure surrounded by scraggly trees. A man came running out of the house followed by two small children. The three of them climbed into an old pickup truck and headed off down the single-lane dirt road in the direction of the airfield. By the time the Cessna was circling the airport and preparing to land, the pickup had arrived at the airfield. But the passengers in the pickup weren't the only ones there. About three hundred people were gathered on the airfield waiting to welcome Mrs. Ruten and her new baby.

"You must be a popular lady!" Betty exclaimed. "We'll have to wait until someone on the ground clears everyone off the runway."

As she spoke, an official strolled out, blew a whistle, and moved the crowd to the side of the runway.

When Betty was convinced it was safe, she began her final approach for landing. The Cessna's wheels touched down together, and the plane rolled to an easy stop. Soon the cockpit was surrounded by eager faces, and it was not until Mrs. Ruten had stepped out and shown everyone the new baby that things began to return to normal.

Betty climbed out of the cockpit and set about unloading Mrs. Ruten's luggage. Mrs. Ruten's husband came over to help. "Thank you so much," he said, glowing. "You don't know what it means to have my wife and new baby back safely."

Betty smiled and glanced over at Mrs. Ruten, who was holding the baby in the center of a crush of admiring Africans while her two other children clung to her legs.

"Would you like to spend the rest of the day with us and fly back tomorrow?" Mr. Ruten asked, lifting a box of supplies from the plane.

"I appreciate the offer, but I have work to do in Kano, and I'm already two days behind schedule," Betty replied.

As she flew the three legs of the trip back to Kano, Betty thought about the missionary work that remained to be done in Nigeria and about the friends she'd made and the ways she had served missionaries across the region. But time was running short for her now. In just three more months her time of service in Nigeria would be over, and she would be heading back to MAF headquarters in California.

Chapter 13

Permission Is Granted

Christmas 1952 was everything Betty imagined it would be. The Greene family gathered at her parents' home in Seattle. Betty's twin brother, Bill, and his family had traveled there from Chicago, where he worked for the Inland Steel Company. Her older brothers Joe and Al and their families were also in Seattle, where they now lived. After returning from China, Al had joined forces with Joe, and in 1950, they opened a private school called Bellevue Christian School. Al served as principal while Joe continued his duties as a Baptist pastor and helped out with school administration whenever he could. Betty had a wonderful time catching up on all of the news from her brothers, their wives, and her nieces and nephews.

As they sat around the dining table talking and devouring a delicious and plentiful Christmas feast, Ann, Betty's four-year-old niece, asked, "Aunt Betty, are you going off to fly airplanes somewhere else, or are you going to stay here with us?"

Betty smiled down at her dimple-cheeked niece. "I'm not going to be flying for a while, at least not my own airplane. In the new year I'm going to be working in the MAF office again, and later in the year I'll be going on a speaking tour of the United States. I'm going to tell people about missionaries and what they do and how airplanes can help them do their work better and faster. I might even meet some pilots who want to join us."

The eyes of her eleven-year-old nephew Norman lit up. "Tell us about the Sahara Desert, Aunt Betty. Is it true it takes a camel a month to trek across it?"

"Yes, it's true," Betty replied.

"Have you ridden on a camel? We studied them in Sunday school," interrupted Ann.

Betty spent the rest of the day answering questions and telling her nieces and nephews all about life in Nigeria and the southern Sahara Desert.

At the end of January 1953, Betty packed up her belongings and once again headed for Los Angeles. In early fall, after several months of working in the office, she set out on a goodwill tour of the United States. She spoke at missions conferences in churches, on university campuses, and in Sunday schools. Many people were interested in the work of MAF, and before she returned to MAF headquarters, Betty had recruited several men who would become strong members of MAF in the years to come. One of them was Bob Lehnhart, who worked with MAF in Brazil and then served as MAF's personnel director.

By the time Betty finally got back to Los Angeles, MAF had moved its headquarters to a new location next to Fullerton Airport. It was a six-acre site that had previously been an orange grove. On it MAF had built an office, a maintenance facility, and a large hangar. As Betty toured the new facility, she marveled at how spacious it was, especially when compared to the tiny office she had started in eight years before in downtown Los Angeles.

Betty threw herself back into her work at the new office. She was busy and happy, and before long it was time for her to head back to Seattle for another family Christmas.

It was not until 1956, three years after returning from Nigeria, that Betty finally took up another overseas assignment with MAF. In late 1955, Betty had been hosting Stuart King and his American wife, Phyllis. Stuart was the director of Missionary Aviation Fellowship in the United Kingdom (MAF-UK), the sister organization of MAF in the United States. The Kings were on their way back to the Sudan in northern Africa after a furlough in England. As Betty told them about her flying experiences in Nigeria, Stuart King came up with an idea. "How would you like to come to the Sudan next year? One of our pilots is due to go on furlough, and we desperately need someone with experience to replace him. Would you consider coming and taking his place?" he asked.

Betty's heart raced. She was always ready to consider a flying assignment.

"But what about the regulations?" Phyllis asked her husband.

"I hadn't considered them. Yes, they could be a problem," he replied in a serious tone. He turned to Betty and in his clipped English accent explained the problem. "As you know, the Sudan has an Islamic government, and it prohibits women from all sorts of careers and work. One of their laws states that no woman is to fly an airplane in Sudanese airspace."

"Do you think they might make an exception for me?" Betty asked. "They do support the work of MAF, don't they?"

"You're right," Stuart agreed. "We have made many humanitarian flights for the Sudanese, and it hasn't gone unnoticed by the government. I could apply for special permission for you to fly in the Sudan. Give me a copy of your resume, and I'll see what I can do."

Betty discussed the new opportunity for service with her old friend and MAF leader Grady Parrott. Both of them agreed that if the government in the Sudan gave Betty permission to fly in their airspace, she should go and do it.

It wasn't long before Betty had her answer. Six weeks later, Stuart King wrote back to Betty. As soon as he had returned to the Sudan, he had begun talking to government officials about the best way to get Betty into the Sudan as a pilot. One official had told him to apply to the Civil Aviation Department for a pilot's license for her and enclose a special letter with the application explaining Betty's qualifications and flying achievements. That's exactly what he did. When Stuart went back to check on the status of the application three weeks later, a beaming official announced, "Permission is granted for the lady pilot to come." Stuart wasn't sure whether it was Betty's being the first woman to fly over the Andes, her wartime flying record, or the eighteen months she'd spent flying in Nigeria that had impressed the officials the most and swayed their decision in her favor.

Betty was delighted with the outcome. She had prayed that if God wanted her to go to the Sudan, He would show it by opening the door for her to fly there. That's just what He had done. Now it was time for her to start thinking about preparing for the Sudan. What to take with her was no problem, but as a pilot, Betty was concerned that she would be ready to fly the particular airplanes flown by MAF in the Sudan.

Stuart King had told Betty she would start out flying a twin-engine De Havilland Rapide, but MAF-UK was in the process of buying the latest model Cessna 180 with a single 230-horsepower engine. Betty wasn't familiar with the Rapide, and since it was a new airplane, she had no experience with the Cessna 180. Before she could feel confident going to the Sudan, she needed some experience flying both aircraft.

Hobey Lowrance, a pilot working at MAF headquarters in Fullerton, had access to a twin-engine Cessna, which he assured Betty handled very much like a Rapide. He took her up flying for several hours until she felt comfortable at the controls. An opportunity also arose for Betty to ferry a new Cessna 180 from the Wichita, Kansas, factory where the plane was manufactured to Colorado Springs. Betty loved the feel of the Cessna in the air and looked forward to flying one in the Sudan.

In Colorado Springs, she visited Dawson and Lila Trotman, who had moved there from Los Angeles. They all had a wonderful reunion, whiling away the hours reliving old times. Betty still appreciated how kind and supportive Dawson had been to MAF ten years earlier when the organization was comprised of just herself, Jim Truxton, and Grady Parrott, with nothing more than a dream and an old typewriter. Betty filled the Trotmans in on her new flying assignment in the Sudan. As she told them that she would be leaving in six weeks—right after the new year, 1956—she had no idea of the tragedy about to strike MAF.

It was Monday, January 8, 1956. As Betty was pouring herself a cup of morning coffee at the MAF office, she glanced out the window to see Grady Parrott walking grimly around the corner of the building. She knew Grady well enough to know something was very wrong.

The office door swung open, and Grady strode in. "Sit down, Betty," he said. "It's bad news."

"What is it?" Betty asked, her mind racing with possibilities.

"It's Nate Saint in Ecuador. I got a phone call in the middle of the night from a ham radio operator in Los Angeles. He had picked up a message for us from Quito. Apparently Nate flew four missionaries into Auca territory, and now all of them are missing." He stopped a moment to clear his throat. Betty noticed large tears collecting at the edge of his eyelids. Grady brushed the tears with the back of his hand and then said in a husky voice, "They've spotted the Piper Cruiser from the air, but it's been stripped of its outer skin. I'm going down there to see what I can do to help."

"But what happened?" Betty asked, her mind scrambling to absorb the news Grady had just delivered. "Did he crash the plane?"

"No, the plane wasn't crashed. He was ferrying four men into the area when they all disappeared. At least I think that's what's happened. The ham radio operator didn't know any more. But it looks bad."

"Shall I come with you?" Betty asked.

"No, it would be good if you could stay here and hold down the fort. I think there's something really wrong, and I'd feel a whole lot better knowing you were here dealing with the media and everything else."

Betty nodded, thinking about the best way to cancel her plans to go to the Sudan the following week.

That night, Betty tossed and turned in bed, praying for Nate Saint and the four other men who were missing. She thought about the first time she met the blue-eyed, blond-haired pilot with the ready smile and willing attitude. Nate Saint had been the person who'd come down to Mexico to rebuild the Waco biplane after the crash at El Real. He never complained, not even when the job took five times longer than anticipated. Nate and his new wife, Marj, had volunteered to work with MAF at a remote station in the middle of the Ecuadorian jungle. They'd had three children there and established a reputation for themselves as being a hospitable, fun-loving family.

The next morning Betty waited for news of Nate and the other missionaries. The situation did not look good. The yellow Piper Cruiser Nate was flying had been abandoned on a lonely strip of sand beside the Curaray River, where it had been stripped of its canvas skin and vandalized. There was no sign of the men. "Palm Beach," as the small strip of sand had been nicknamed by the missionaries, was inside the territory of the infamous Auca Indians. Even in the Amazon jungle, where many tribes practiced head-hunting and ritual killing, the Aucas were feared and avoided by other tribes. They had a reputation for killing anyone who came into their territory, and they waged bloody battles against each other. Betty, like most others who knew the situation, had grave fears about the men's safety in such an inhospitable environment.

By week's end, everyone's worst fears were realized. A helicopter from the U.S. Air Force base in Panama had spotted bodies in the water, and a rescue party made up of Ecuadorian soldiers and local missionaries had trekked into the jungle and found four of the five missing men's bodies. The men had been speared to death. The bodies were buried under a tree at the end of Palm Beach.

News of the "mid-century martyrs," as the men had been dubbed, soon made its way around the world. *Life* magazine sent its top photographer, Cornell Capa, to cover the story. Meanwhile, the phone at MAF headquarters rang off the hook with newspaper reporters wanting background details on Nate Saint or churches wanting MAF to know how much they cared and that they were praying for everyone.

Ten days later, Grady Parrott returned to California and reported on the situation in Ecuador. All five of the widows were determined to continue serving God in some way, and for the time being, Nate Saint's wife, Marj, had decided to stay on in the jungle and man the radio and help Johnny Keenan, MAF's second pilot there, carry out the increased workload. MAF promised to send another pilot as soon as possible.

Betty, like everyone else in MAF, was greatly affected by the tragedy. Nate Saint was MAF's first worker to lose his life in the course of carrying out his duties, and people wondered whether stricter MAF guidelines or policies might have saved his life. They would never know for sure.

Some good did come out of the deaths of the five missionaries, however. The widespread coverage in magazines such as *Time* and *Life* meant that just about anyone in the world who kept up with the news had heard about the deaths. Many Christians asked themselves whether they were willing to lay down their lives to take the gospel message to tribes who had never heard it before. Over the next decade, thousands of young people dedicated themselves to becoming missionaries in response to the story of the deaths of the five young men in the South American jungle.

By April 1956, Betty felt things had calmed down enough in the MAF office for her to leave for the Sudan. She booked passage on the S.S. *America,* which sailed from New York to Southampton, England. She had never been on a long ocean voyage before, and it made her appreciate the role of airplanes in getting people to places fast.

Once in England she spent three days in London being briefed for her new assignment in the Sudan. After the briefing, she boarded a commercial airplane to fly to Cairo, Egypt. From there she took another flight on to Khartoum, the Sudanese capital. And from there she flew on to Malakal, where she was to be stationed.

Chapter 14

The Sudan

The sun blazed down on Betty as she unfolded her long legs and climbed from the small commercial aircraft. She was glad to be out of the cramped passenger cabin and finally standing in Malakal, a city perched on the edge of the Nile River with a population of about seven thousand people. Waiting to greet her were Stuart and Phyllis King, along with Milton and Peggy Thompson, the missionary couple she would be staying with until the new MAF house was completed. They all welcomed Betty to Malakal, and Milton helped get her papers in order for the customs and immigration officers.

Once all the official details had been taken care of, the Thompsons drove Betty past the MAF hangar at the edge of the airport. Betty could see the De

Havilland Rapide through the open doors. The craft was a large twin-engine biplane with room in its cabin for eight passengers and plenty of luggage.

The following morning, Betty awoke refreshed and anxious to get to work. At 9 A.M. Gordon Marshall, the South African pilot she would be replacing, arrived to take her up for her first flight in the Rapide. By 11 A.M. she was soaring through the skies above Malakal. She found the Rapide remarkably easy to handle for its size, and the visibility from the cockpit was good. As Betty familiarized herself with the controls and various instrument settings, Gordon explained about the work of MAF-UK in the area. The organization served 150 missionary families, most of them located at remote outposts that were days away by truck from any sizable towns where they could find medical help, buy supplies, or send their children to school. Indeed, most of the children attended boarding schools in Addis Ababa, Ethiopia, or in Egypt, and MAF was kept busy at the beginning and end of school vacations ferrying children to and from their homes. Since there were so few airplanes in the area, MAF also flew government officials around when the need arose. The officials paid regular commercial fares on such flights.

One of Betty's first flying assignments in the Sudan was to fly three government officials to El Renk and back. El Renk was an ancient city located 175 miles north on the banks of the Nile. Betty got an early start and took a book with her to read while waiting for the officials to conduct their business at the airport in El Renk. By lunchtime, the men hadn't finished. Just as Betty was beginning to wonder what she should do for lunch, one of the officials came into the airport passenger lounge where she was waiting and asked, "Would you like to have lunch with us?"

Betty was a little unsure of what the man exactly meant. Although she had not been in the Sudan long, she'd had time to observe that there were big differences between Islamic men and women. The women wore long dresses with veils covering most of their face. Men, on the other hand, dressed like Westerners in long pants and shirts. The men and women didn't interact much. And they especially never ate together. So the official's invitation to have lunch with a group of Islamic men took Betty by surprise.

Betty followed the official to a small military building located at the edge of the airport, all the while wondering what she might be in for. When they reached the building, the official opened the door for her. As her eyes adjusted from the bright glare of the midday sun outside to the low level of light in the room, Betty could make out five men sitting around a table. There were two empty places at the table.

"Please, sit down and join us, Captain Greene," the official said, pulling a chair out for her.

Betty was surprised. She was actually going to sit at the same table with the men and eat with them.

The food was delicious. The first course was a green dip served with fresh baked bread. It was followed by roast chicken and a huge platter of fresh fruit to finish off. At first they all ate in silence, but as the men began to feel comfortable around Betty, they started asking her questions. Did many women fly in America? How did she learn to fly? Where had she flown before? And just as they were starting in on the fruit platter, the question Betty had been waiting for was asked. "What is it that made you come to the Sudan as a pilot?"

Betty smiled and began to tell the men about how she had dreamed of combining her two great interests in life, her love of flying and her love of God, into a single career. She had found a way to combine them in the Missionary Aviation Fellowship, which she had helped found. And like her, there were now other pilots in other countries around the world who had also combined these two loves and were doing the same thing as she was: helping make the work of missionaries easier by transporting them where they needed to go and keeping them stocked with supplies. The Sudanese men were impressed with her answer and thanked her for sharing the meal with them.

As she flew the men back to Malakal, Betty thought about the unique opportunities being a female pilot gave her. Flying opened many doors to sharing the gospel message with people that were often closed to regular missionaries.

Several weeks later, Betty had another experience that was much more typically Sudanese. She was logging her flight plan when Said Hilmi, Malakal Airport's chief officer, walked up to her. "Ah, Captain Greene, it is so good to see you this lovely morning. It is a good day for flying," he said.

Betty nodded and gave him a smile.

"I would like to invite you to a celebration at my house. My baby son is about to turn forty days old, and it is our custom to have a party then. The governor, deputy governor, and chief of police will all be attending, and I would be honored to have you come too," Said Hilmi said.

"Thank you. That would be wonderful. I flew the governor to Khartoum recently, and I look forward to meeting him again," Betty replied.

Said Hilmi gave Betty a strange look before giving her the details of how to get to his house. He gave her an invitation for fellow pilot Ernie Krenzin and his wife, Doreen, to attend as well. The Krenzins were an American couple who had recently arrived in the Sudan to fly with MAF.

As the night of the celebration approached, Betty wondered what she should wear. After all, it was the biggest social event she had been invited to in the Sudan so far. She settled on a light blue linen suit with cream piping and buttons.

Doreen Krenzin dressed up for the occasion as well, and she and Betty laughed as they walked together in their finery to MAF's old pickup truck for the drive to Said Hilmi's home. Betty was surprised by his house, which was much more lavish than she had imagined it would be.

Ernie dropped the two women off at the front gate and went to park the pickup. Said Hilmi was waiting inside to greet them. "Welcome. I am so glad you could come," he said in his excellent English. "Please, follow Nada," he added, gesturing toward a woman covered from head to toe in her traditional Islamic dress.

Betty and Doreen followed the woman up a central staircase, through a room in which all manner of mouthwatering food was laid out on long tables, and onto a balcony. The woman then opened a door and led them into a long dormitory-like room with six single beds lined up neatly against the far wall. A woman was perched on the end of one of the beds.

With the door shut firmly behind them, Betty and Doreen looked at each other. The woman sitting on the bed beckoned for them to sit with her. With the use of hand signals and the tiny bit of Arabic she could speak, Betty was able to learn that the woman was Said Hilmi's wife. Soon other women arrived, each one wearing the same long garb and veil. They greeted each other and spoke rapidly in Arabic, laughing as they did so. Betty wished she could speak more Arabic. None of the women could speak any English, since women were not permitted to go to school or learn other languages.

After an hour had passed, the door to the room swung open again, and Nada walked in carrying

Said Hilmi's baby son. The women all began speaking excitedly, and they all wanted to hold the baby at once. Betty got to hold him for a while, too.

After holding and admiring the baby, Betty assumed they would all be joining in the celebration with the other guests. Instead another hour dragged on until Nada reappeared at the door and made an announcement. The Sudanese women, who had been half sitting and half lying on the beds, sprang to their feet. Betty also stood up and straightened her linen jacket. She and Doreen followed the others out onto the balcony, where a table laden with food had been set up. The Sudanese women all sat down, making room for Betty and Doreen, and began to eat. The meal seemed to last forever, and Betty began to despair about getting to mingle with any of the other guests. To Betty's dismay, when the meal was over, Nada gestured for Betty and Doreen to follow her. She led them back downstairs and outside to where Ernie Krenzin was waiting for them by the pickup truck.

Apart from Said Hilmi, Betty had seen no other man throughout the whole celebration. She had been kept separate with the women of the household. And while she didn't like it one bit, she knew it was the normal course of events for women in the Sudan, unlike the lunch she'd enjoyed with the male government officials at the airport in El Renk.

Betty spent five months flying the De Havilland Rapide before word finally came that the replacement Cessna 180 was waiting in England. There was just one catch: The plane had been shipped from the United States in pieces, and it needed to be assembled. MAF-UK decided that Betty should fly the Rapide to England, where it could be sold, and when the Cessna 180 was finally assembled, she could fly it back to the Sudan. Stuart and Phyllis King and their two-year-old daughter Becky accompanied Betty on the trip. Phyllis was expecting another baby and wanted it to be born in England. As well, Stuart would be able to help reassemble the Cessna. He had served in the Royal Air Force during World War II, not as a pilot but as an airplane mechanic. Indeed it was Stuart's skill at fixing aircraft that had kept the Rapide flying safely all over the Sudan.

The four of them took off on their four-thousand-mile journey to England on August 10, 1956. As Betty prepared the Rapide for the flight early that morning, she saw the local air traffic controller unlocking the door to the control tower. "Today is the big day?" he called. "And it looks as though you've got great weather to fly."

"Yes," Betty replied. "I'm just checking everything one last time, especially the long-range fuel tanks."

"You will be back, won't you?" the controller asked.

"Yes," Betty said with a smile, "but not with this plane. We are going to replace it with a new Cessna. I should be back with it by October or November at the latest."

"We'll all be following your progress," the air traffic controller said, opening the door to the control tower and then adding before stepping inside, "If you need anything, you can count on us."

On the first day of the journey, Betty flew the Rapide north above the Nile to Wadi Halfa, located on the border between Egypt and the Sudan. There they spent the first night. Early the next morning they took off on the next leg of their journey, which would take them to Cairo, with a refueling stop at Asyut along the way. Next they would fly on to Mersa Matruk on Egypt's Mediterranean coast, where they planned to spend their second night. By 1:45 P.M. the Rapide was flying over the great pyramids and was soon safely on the ground at Cairo Airport for another refueling stop. All went well on the journey until they attempted to get permission to land at Mersa Matruk. Stuart King, who was operating the Rapide's clunky radio on the trip for Betty, had tried several times to inform the airport at Mersa Matruk that they were ready to land. But there was no reply.

It was then that Betty realized how closely the air traffic controllers back in the Sudan were following her journey. Two minutes after getting no reply from the airport at Mersa Matruk, a crackly voice came over the radio. "Rapide Victor Papa King Charlie Victor, this is Khartoum. We have picked up your message and will relay it for you. Over."

Betty looked at Stuart. The controller was twelve hundred miles away in Khartoum, but he had been monitoring their frequency the whole time, just in case they needed help. Betty smiled in amazement at how kind these staunchly Muslim men were toward a group of Christian missionaries.

"Roger, Khartoum. This is Rapide VP-KCV. Please advise Mersa Matruk airport we will be landing in twenty minutes. Thank you. Over and out," Stuart replied into the radio microphone.

Betty was glad when the airplane finally touched down at the airport. It had been a long day. She had flown for eight and a half hours over unfamiliar territory, causing her to pay close attention to her maps each step of the way.

The following morning they got another early start. Betty guided the Rapide westward along the Mediterranean coast to Banina, located on the eastern side of the Gulf of Sidra in Libya. From there she headed in a straight line for Tripoli, Libya's capital. This meant flying over the Gulf of Sidra for two hours, during which time they were out of sight of land. The Rapide had been outfitted with water survival gear, however, just in case something went wrong.

The following day was Sunday, and they spent it resting in Tripoli. On Monday morning it was back into the airplane. This time they headed out over the Mediterranean Sea in a northwesterly direction toward Tunis, located at the northeastern tip of Tunisia. There they stopped for lunch and to refuel before heading due north for Ajaccio on the island of Corsica, tucked between France and Italy on the other side of the Mediterranean Sea. That night they ate dinner at the Napoleon Restaurant in Ajaccio, named in honor of Napoleon Bonaparte, the famous French general who was born on Corsica.

On Tuesday morning Betty flew the Rapide on to Lyon, France, where they spent the night and prepared for the final leg of their journey, 430 miles north to Croydon, England.

Having never piloted an airplane into England before, Betty looked for large landmarks to guide her. Crossing the English Channel, she spotted the white cliffs of Dover, made famous by a wartime song. She knew exactly where she was as she crossed over them and began following a railway track that led her all the way to Croydon, a large suburb at the southern edge of London.

"Rapide Victor Papa King Charlie Victor, you are cleared for landing," came a voice over the radio.

Betty smiled at Stuart King seated beside her.

"We made it!" Stuart said. "All four thousand miles of it. How many hours did it take?"

Betty looked at her watch. "I'd say just about thirty-nine hours," she said, "though I'll have to add it up in the logbook when we land."

A group of cheering well-wishers was waiting for them at Croydon Airport, and they were soon whisked away to the Foreign Missions Club, where they were to stay until the Cessna 180 was ready.

Betty found plenty to keep her busy. She prepared the De Havilland Rapide for sale and attended a missions conference in York, where she did what she loved most, talking to young people about using their talents to help spread the gospel message. However, there was a holdup with the Cessna, and it was not until just before Christmas 1956 that the crates containing the plane were finally released by British Customs.

Both Betty and Stuart King were concerned for the missionaries in the Sudan, since they had been without air service for several months now. They both hoped that the Cessna could be put together in about a week and be flying in the Sudan by early February. The Kings abandoned their holiday plans, and Stuart and Betty stood ready to work nonstop assembling the airplane.

It was an exciting moment as the first crate was jimmied open in the Hunting Clan Airways hangar at Heathrow Airport. But the mood soon turned to shock when Betty and Stuart realized that the wings and undercarriage had been taken apart without anyone labeling the parts. Putting the plane back together without the parts being labeled was going to take much longer than planned, especially since neither of them was particularly familiar with the Cessna 180. Despite the setback, they went to work. A month later, the plane finally was in one piece, had been inspected, and was ready to fly.

By now it was nearly the end of January 1957, and another problem, which had nothing to do with the Cessna, had arisen. During October 1956, a war between Great Britain and France and Egypt had erupted. Egypt had gained control of the Suez Canal and intended to nationalize it, using the money earned from running the canal to finance construction of the Aswan High Dam on the Nile River. Great Britain and France opposed Egypt's action and sent troops to invade the country under the guise of assuring the safe passage of ships through the Suez Canal. In response the Egyptians sank forty ships in the canal, blocking it completely. The United Nations intervened in the fighting, and a truce was established in November. The British and French troops were then withdrawn. However, given the tense situation in the area, there was no way Betty could fly back over Egypt to the Sudan following the route she had come. She would have to map out another course to get her back to Malakal.

Betty weighed things carefully and eventually decided the best way back to the Sudan was to fly down the coast of West Africa and then swing east inland to Malakal. It was twice as long as the other route, but it was safe. Betty filed her flight plan at the Civil Aviation office in London. She was promptly told by a Mr. Fuquay, the office director, that in his opinion it was madness to fly a small, single-engine airplane over such a route, and he would not approve the flight plan. Betty was surprised and disappointed. She had not expected to be turned down, and the rebuff would delay her return to the Sudan.

Betty decided that the best way to overcome Mr. Fuquay's objections to her flight plan was to present him with enough information to make him change his mind. She set to work typing him a three-page letter outlining the work of MAF, the flying experience she'd had, and the safety equipment and features of the airplane. Finally, after two weeks of waiting, she received word that Mr. Fuquay had relented and approved her plan.

On Friday, March 1, 1957, five people—Betty, Stuart and Phyllis King, their daughter Becky, and their new baby, John—crowded into the Cessna 180. After takeoff, Betty headed the plane toward Paris and then on to Bordeaux in the south of France, where they spent their first night. The next day they continued on to Madrid, Spain, and then to Tangier, Morocco, on the northern tip of the African continent. From Tangier they hugged the coastline to Casablanca and on to the port town of Dakhia, Western Sahara. The next day they continued south along the coast to Saint Louis in northern Senegal, and then to Freetown, Sierra Leone, and Monrovia, Liberia.

As they reached Monrovia, the halfway point of the eight-thousand-mile journey back to the Sudan, it was time to take a break from traveling. Phyllis King had a lot of diaper washing to catch up on, and Becky needed time to burn off some energy after sitting and playing quietly on the floor of the Cessna hour after hour. They spent two days in Monrovia. The break suited Betty well. Her missionary friends the de la Hayes were now stationed in Monrovia, and Betty visited and stayed with them. Her first night there, the de la Hayes invited Betty to go along with them to a special reception for American Vice President Richard Nixon and his wife, who were visiting West Africa. The reception was lavish, the best the government of Liberia could put together, and Betty enjoyed the evening very much.

On Saturday the five travelers clambered back into the Cessna as they headed farther around the coast of West Africa and on to the Gulf of Guinea. That night they landed in Lagos, Nigeria. The next day they flew across the delta of the Niger River and down the coasts of Cameroon and French Equatorial Africa (now Gabon). Here Betty left the coast and headed eastward to Leopoldville (now called Kinshasa), the Congo (now Zaire). From there they flew north over the Congo to Juba, in southern Sudan. And from there they made the final leg of the trip back to Malakal.

On Thursday, March 14, 1957, two weeks after leaving London and eight thousand miles later, Betty touched the silver Cessna 180 down on the runway at its new home base, Malakal, the Sudan. Soon she was back flying her regular rounds, serving the missionaries on the ground.

Chapter 15

New Guinea

Betty sat in the MAF office in Fullerton, California, studying the map of New Guinea laid out on the desk in front of her. After Greenland, New Guinea was the world's second largest island. The shape of the island on the map resembled a great dinosaur perched above the northernmost tip of Australia. The dinosaur's head rested on the equator, and its tail descended all the way into the Coral Sea. Two lines divided the island into three parts. The first line ran north and south through the center. The territory it created to the west was called Dutch New Guinea (now Irian Jaya), which had been administered by the Dutch since 1828. A second line running east and west through the eastern portion of the island divided it into the Territory of

165

New Guinea in the north and Papua in the south. Before World War I, the Territory of New Guinea had belonged to Germany, but now Australia administered both of these eastern sectors.

In the northeastern corner of Dutch New Guinea lay the town of Sentani, which was going to be the base for Betty's next flying assignment with MAF. Leaving the Sudan in October 1958 after two and a half years of flying there, Betty spent the next eighteen months working at MAF's headquarters in Fullerton, California. But in June 1960, she was scheduled to replace pilot Paul Pontier, who had been serving in Sentani and was returning home on furlough.

The work of MAF had been growing rapidly in New Guinea, partly as a result of the increased public awareness stirred up by Marj Saint, who had undertaken a speaking tour of Australia and New Zealand. Marj talked about her husband Nate's death at the hands of the Auca Indians in Ecuador and went on to tell of the many opportunities for missionary service that existed and that needed to be taken up by Christians.

Many people responded to Marj Saint's appeal, and both workers and donations poured into MAF. As a result, four MAF pilots and planes were now flying in New Guinea. Originally the work there had been started by the Australian branch of MAF. In 1951, however, MAF-Australia's most experienced pilot, Harry Hartwig, had crashed his single-engine Auster airplane, killing himself and destroying the aircraft. Following this tragic accident, MAF-Australia had invited MAF-US to join it in serving the missionaries scattered throughout the country.

Betty was excited about her new assignment; it reminded her of when she was in Peru. Indeed there were many parallels between the two areas. The Amazon jungle and the highlands of New Guinea were two of the most unexplored places on Earth. Many areas of New Guinea were unmapped, and no one knew for sure all that lay inland. It had been only eight years since Grady Parrott had been granted permission by the government of Dutch New Guinea to be the first pilot to fly over some of the eastern inland areas. What Grady saw there stunned everyone. In an area that most geographers assumed to be unpopulated, Grady spotted the Dani people, all 150,000 of them! The people were living in stone age fashion in small village groupings. Even now, eight years later, there was still much to learn about New Guinea and its inhabitants.

When Betty arrived, she found New Guinea to be all she had expected, and more. The contrast between areas was breathtaking. Towering high mountains were wrapped in endless veils of clouds, huge rivers gushed through rocky canyons and dense tropical forests, and ubiquitous coconut palms fringed golden beaches.

MAF's three other pilots, George Boggs, David Steiger, and Bob Johanson, welcomed Betty to New Guinea. Soon after her arrival, Betty was given a Cessna 180 to fly and put to work. Just as in the

Sudan and Peru, there were food and supplies to ferry into mission stations, sick missionaries and locals to fly out, and a host of other routine duties.

In November, five months after arriving in New Guinea, Betty heard about a new airstrip that was soon to be opened. A pioneering missionary couple, Bill and Grace Cutts, were working among the Moni people in the remote village of Hitadipa. Betty had met the Cuttses when they were stationed at Homejo, another Moni village, and liked them very much. But now new missionaries had been trained to carry on the work there, and the Cuttses had moved farther inland to open up new areas of Moni territory to the gospel message.

It was in Hitadipa that the new airstrip had been constructed, and this airstrip would provide Bill and Grace Cutts a more convenient way in and out of the area. Otherwise it required a three-day trek over steep terrain just to get to the village. However, MAF had a strict policy that one of its pilots must inspect any new airstrip before an MAF plane could land there. The fact that this new airstrip at Hitadipa needed to be inspected gave Betty an idea: Perhaps she should be the pilot to do it.

One day soon afterward she found Dave Steiger alone at Sentani and asked him, "I was wondering if you would consider letting me be the pilot who inspects the new airstrip at Hitadipa."

David Steiger looked at Betty, his eyes grave. "It's a thirty-five-mile trek there," he said. "And it's over rugged terrain. It will take whoever goes to

inspect the airstrip at least three days to get there."
He paused for a long moment, his eyes scanning
Betty. "Are you sure that's what you want to do?"

Betty nodded deliberately. "I've talked to Leona
St. John, who's stationed at Homejo, and she says
she'll go with me."

"It sounds to me as though you've thought this
all out. I guess if that's what you want to do, I can
arrange it for you."

"Thank you," Betty replied.

"It's quite a task you've set for yourself. I hope
you're still thanking me when you get to Hitadipa,"
David Steiger added.

"I hope so, too," smiled Betty.

True to his word, David Steiger arranged everything, and in early December, Betty found herself
on the way to Homejo. The airstrip there was
perched on a rocky ledge halfway up the side of a
mountain and was angled uphill. This meant that
the Cessna would stop in a very short distance,
which was a good thing, since there was a sheer
drop into a canyon at the end of the runway. As
George Boggs, who was flying Betty in, circled the
Cessna around the airstrip, Leona St. John and a fellow missionary came running out onto the runway
with an old white sheet. They held two corners each
and allowed the sheet to billow in the wind, making
a primitive windsock. Once George had established
the direction and approximate speed of the wind
from the windsock, he brought the Cessna in for a
perfect landing.

As soon as the plane's engine had stopped, Leona opened the cockpit door for Betty. "Hello. How was the flight?" she asked.

"Wonderful," Betty replied. "How about things here? Is everything going on schedule?"

Leona grinned. "Ahead, actually," she said. "Our eight guides have gone on ahead. They left at day-break, and we're hoping they'll be waiting for us at Pogapa."

Betty climbed out of the cockpit to allow Leona to get herself and her backpack into the rear seat of the airplane.

Soon they were back in the air, headed to Pogapa airstrip located ten minutes flying time farther up the valley. As they approached the airstrip, Betty could understand why it had the reputation of being the most difficult airstrip in the country. It sat sixty-one hundred feet up on a mountain plateau, with steep slopes leading to deep ravines on three sides. The strip itself at nine hundred feet in length was barely adequate, making any landing or takeoff a heart-stopping event. George Boggs eased the Cessna over the landing strip as all three of them searched the ground for any logs or rocks that might flip the plane over if it hit them. Satisfied there were none, George lined the plane up for a landing. This time there were no missionaries holding up a makeshift windsock for him to gauge wind speed and direction. Instead he studied the way the trees around the landing strip were swaying, which gave him some idea of wind direction.

Again George made a perfect landing. After he had touched down, he taxied the Cessna over to an unoccupied mission house. Betty could see the eight guides beside the old house waving at them.

"Dugulugu and his men made it in good time!" Leona St. John exclaimed. "It's good to have such reliable guides with us."

As soon as the Cessna's engine had stopped, Betty, Leona, and George climbed out of the plane. Leona talked to the men in the Moni language for a minute or two and then reached into the back of the plane and retrieved her backpack.

"Everything is fine," she told Betty. "They're eager to get going."

Meanwhile, George Boggs unloaded Betty's backpack before walking around the Cessna to check that everything was fine for the return flight. "Well, ladies, I guess you're on your own," he finally said.

After saying a short prayer for the group, George climbed back into the cockpit of the Cessna. He glanced at the oil pressure and gas gauges as the plane's engine burst into life. The two women and the group of native men watched as the plane bounced along the rough airstrip and then climbed into the air. When the plane had disappeared from view over a mountain ridge, Betty and Leona helped each other hoist their backpacks onto their backs.

"Okay, let's get going," Leona said.

Betty went last as they set off up the trail. She studied her traveling companions as they walked past her. They were typical New Guinea highland men, dressed only with a string around their waist. They all had the same thick, dark, almost woolly hair, and each man was only about five feet tall. Three of the men carried the equipment to start out with. The others would take over the load farther along the trail. The first man carried the food box, which rested on his back and was held in place by a strap from his forehead. Betty marveled at the strength the man must have in his neck and upper back to carry the box. The second man carried the tent, and the third had sleeping bags and camping supplies suspended on his back. Betty and Leona carried their own personal items and a change of clothes in their backpacks.

As the last reverberations of the Cessna's engine faded, a sense of isolation washed over Betty as she stood on the side of a mountain in hostile territory in the highlands of New Guinea. Anything could happen in the next three days. There was the possibility of physical injury. If any member of the team broke a leg or suffered some other serious injury, it would take days to get help. And then there was the threat of being ambushed. Betty had been told that the tribes in the highlands were in a state of constant war with each other. The tribes believed that no one died by accident, so if someone did die, it was because some enemy had put a curse on the person. Thus, when a death in a village occurred, warriors were sent out to make someone "pay" for it. This kept the highlands in a state of upheaval, and it was the main reason Bill and Grace Cutts had moved to Hitadipa. The couple wanted to show the Moni people that there was a better way to live.

Dugulugu, the lead native guide, pointed downward and said some words in the Moni language. Leona St. John nodded and turned to Betty. "He says the first thing we need to do is go down to the bottom of the hill and cross the river. There's a vine bridge there."

Betty smiled and nodded. "Lead on," she said.

Just getting to the bottom of the hill proved hard work, and Betty began to wonder what she had let herself in for. Finally a river emerged from the thick jungle undergrowth. And there was the vine bridge Dugulugu had told them about. Betty took a deep breath when she saw the flimsy structure. A tangle of intertwined vines about two inches thick formed the "deck" of the bridge; two more vines strung higher up were handrails. Other vines were zigzagged between the deck and the handrails to hold them together.

Leona looked at Betty and said, "This is supposed to be one of the best kept bridges in the area. No one has fallen off it in quite a while."

Betty smiled weakly. She was not afraid of heights, but when she went up in an airplane, she made sure everything was as safe as it could possibly be. Now she was about to venture out onto a bridge constructed of vines, and she had no way of telling whether or not it was safe.

Dugulugu, who had taken over carrying the box of food, was the first to cross the footbridge. Betty watched as his wide feet almost curved themselves around the vines as he walked. She looked down at her boots and wondered whether she would be able to make it across wearing such heavy-soled footwear. Perhaps she ought to try crossing the bridge barefoot herself. Within minutes Dugulugu was safely across and had beckoned for the others to follow. Soon only Leona and Betty were left to cross.

"You go first," Leona said to Betty, "and I'll start across as soon as you reach the other side. At least we know the bridge has been well tested before us."

Well tested, or weakened by the others, Betty wanted to say, but she kept her silence. By now she'd had plenty of time to study the proper crossing technique. You kept your eyes fixed on the far end of the bridge and slowly slid your hands along the vine "rails" with each step you took.

As she took her first steps on the vine bridge, Betty was surprised by how springy it was. She had taken about ten steps and was well out over the swirling river twenty feet below when she heard a snap. She froze in place, her eyes darting from side to side to see what had happened. Several of the zigzag vines that held the handrail vines in place were broken. But had they just broken, or had they been broken all along? Betty couldn't tell, and for the first time in her life she found herself unable to move because of fear. She could keep a clear head and respond when an airplane's engine suddenly stopped in midair, but the thought of going another step on the flimsy bridge terrified her.

As Betty stood clinging tightly to the vine rails, one of the Moni guides began making his way toward her from the far side of the bridge. Betty could feel cold sweat beading on her forehead. The thought of another person on the bridge only heightened her anxiety. Now twice as much weight was on the bridge as before. They were doomed for sure!

Betty watched as the guide nimbly made his way to her. When he reached her, he gently touched her hand and smiled. He then took a step backward and waited for Betty to follow. Betty nodded, knowing what he expected her to do. She slowly slid her right foot along the vine about eight inches, then slid her left foot even with her right foot and slid her left foot another eight inches. She had taken a step! A surge of adrenaline went through her. She knew she could do it now. And so, step by step she followed the Moni guide to the other side, where Dugulugu excitedly patted her on the back, a look of relief on his face.

"I hope there aren't too many more of these," Betty said when Leona finally made it across the bridge to join them.

"Only a couple more, but you know what to expect now," Leona replied. "I was thinking while I watched you cross," she went on. "Last month Grace Cutts got sick and had to walk out for treatment. Can you imagine feeling dizzy and ill and having to walk across that bridge?"

Betty shook her head. There was nothing like walking up and down steep mountains to remind a pilot of why his or her airplane was so valuable to missionaries serving on the ground. The hope was that if all went well with the airstrip inspection at Hitadipa, people would no longer have to make this torturous trek over mountains and through dense jungle. Of course, they had to get to Hitadipa and the airstrip first.

Chapter 16

Hitadipa at Last

At 3 P.M. the two missionary women and their eight guides stopped for lunch. Betty perched on a large, flat rock and devoured a sandwich while rubbing her weary leg muscles. Although she felt tired and sore from all the walking, she noticed the Moni guides seemed to bounce with energy. They looked as though they hadn't walked more than a mile. Betty wished she had their stamina.

Finally Leona St. John announced that it was time to get moving again. The guides leapt to their feet and eagerly loaded up the gear they were carrying on their backs. Betty pulled her backpack on again and followed the Moni guides on up the trail.

The group walked on for another hour and a half through thick rain forest, clambering over the roots of large camphor and ebony trees. Finally, at 4:30 P.M., Leona announced that it was time to make camp for the night. They were within a few hundred yards of a village, which Dugulugu assured them was a friendly one. The guides helped the two women set up their tent, and then they were gone.

"Where are the guides? They haven't deserted us, have they?" Betty asked.

Leona laughed. "No, they've gone into the village for the night. It would be very difficult for them to stay out here with us," she said.

Betty looked a little confused, so Leona explained. "When the sun goes down, they get very cold. They don't wear clothes, and they don't use rugs or blankets when they sleep, so they need to be inside a hut huddled around a fire."

"I see," Betty said. "I hadn't thought about how they would sleep. We're up quite high here. I guess it gets rather cold at night."

The two women ate some canned baked beans and finished their sandwiches from lunch. Then it was time for bed. Before they crawled into the tent, Leona read a psalm while Betty prayed that God would watch over them while they slept.

As she snuggled into her sleeping bag, Betty thought about the airstrip she was going to inspect. All the time and energy that had gone into making it would benefit countless people in the future. That thought alone made each aching muscle and the terrifying experience on the vine bridge worthwhile.

The next morning, Betty and Leona were up bright and early. Just as they were finishing their breakfast, the guides reappeared, and soon everything was repacked and they were on their way again.

They had been walking for an hour and a half when they heard the buzz of an airplane engine. Stepping into a clearing, Betty shielded her eyes from the morning sun. Above them a Cessna was circling. Betty waved, thankful to know that George Boggs was watching out for them.

Soon they reached a spot on a ridge where Betty could look back down the valley they had been climbing through. Far in the distance on the opposite side of the valley she could barely make out the airstrip at Pogapa. It had taken them a day to cover the same distance George Boggs had covered in five minutes of flying.

They walked on in silence, up and over a mountain ridge that was eighty-five hundred feet above sea level. Although it was hard walking to get to the top of the ridge, Betty could not help but be awed by the spectacular view from its summit.

Of course each ridge they climbed meant that they had to clamber down the other side of it. Soon they were slipping and sliding their way down a sixty-degree slope. As they did so, Betty was glad she had decided to wear blue jeans on the trek. At least they gave her legs some protection. She wondered how the Moni men could make it without any form of protective clothing at all.

At the bottom of every ridge, a stream made its way south to join with other streams to form a river that would flow to the Arafura Sea. The river at the bottom of this ridge was particularly beautiful. It was clear and shallow, with tropical foliage draped along its edge. The group sat on a huge fallen log while one of the guides made a small fire to heat some water. The two women enjoyed a steaming cup of coffee and a slab of fruitcake Leona had made before starting on the trek. The Moni men devoured some cold sweet potatoes they had brought with them from the village where they had slept the night before.

Once they had eaten, it was time for them to be on their way again. This time Dugulugu indicated they would walk along the riverbed for a mile or so until they picked up another trail that would take them over the next ridge. Betty's boots proved no protection against the seeping river water, but she did not mind one bit. The river was so peaceful she was glad to spend as much time by it as she could. They trekked on for the rest of the day, and once again as night approached, Dugulugu found them a spot near a friendly village to sleep.

As they approached the site, Betty noticed a wooden platform high up in a tree. "What's that?" she asked, pointing to it.

Leona peered up through the leaves and then said, "We'd better not camp here; that's a death tree. The Moni people put dead bodies up there, and the birds pick the bones clean."

The women camped that night on the far side of the village. Everything went fine, just as it had the night before. Betty arose the next morning refreshed from a good night's sleep and eager to press on with the final leg of the trek. If everything went well on the day's trek, they would be with Bill and Grace Cutts and their baby daughter, Amy, before nightfall.

As they climbed up toward another ridge, they left the lush tropical forest behind and began trekking through tall, well-spaced pine trees. With little undergrowth among these trees, they made good time. At one point, in the distance they could even see the mountain that Hitadipa was situated at the foot of. After going up and over yet another mountain ridge, they came across a village. Leona went ahead to barter with the head man there for some sweet potatoes for the guides to eat. She arrived back fifteen minutes later, her face ashen.

"What's the matter?" Betty asked, knowing immediately that something was wrong.

"War," Leona replied. "Ahead of us, about two villages." She turned to Dugulugu and spoke to him in the Moni language. Then she turned back to Betty. "Dugulugu tells me there is no other trail we can take to Hitadipa. We must keep going the way we planned. We need to pray we don't get caught up in the fighting."

Betty prayed as she nervously walked on. Every cracking twig or muffled sound was investigated lest it be someone trying to ambush them. Finally they reached the top of the next ridge and looked down the other side. A village about a quarter of a mile away was in flames. Betty could hear women and children screaming and caught a glimpse of some warriors with their menacing eight-foot-long spears in hand.

Dugulugu waved his arm toward a large tree, and the two women quickly hid behind it. He joined them there, speaking to Leona in whispers. When he had gone, Leona turned to Betty. "He is going to send two men into the village to see if we will be allowed to pass through safely."

"Even if they say yes, how will we know they're not tricking us?" Betty asked.

"We won't," Leona whispered. "We'll just have to trust their word."

Betty waited anxiously, scanning the trees for any sign of the guides' return. Finally, ten minutes later, the guides arrived back with good news. The attackers had left, and the people of the village were prepared to allow them safe passage.

The village was a sickening sight of broken and burned huts, looted storehouses, and dead bodies. Betty was glad when they were safely through it and again walking in the clean-smelling forest. As they walked on, Leona told her about some of the customs of the Moni people. "There will be a lot more agony before that village gets back to normal," she said.

"Why?" Betty asked.

"Well," Leona sighed, "they like to make sure there's enough grieving for the people who have been killed. They believe a good show of grief helps get the departed ones to the next life. So they round up the young girls in the village, those between ages six and twelve, and chop off their fingers, two or three from each hand. That way they can be sure there will be plenty of weeping and wailing in the village."

Betty felt her stomach turn. "That's terrible," she said. "What about infections?"

Leona shrugged. "Some of the girls die as a result, but they're only females, after all. The wives in the village have it worse. If a man dies in battle, his wife is killed so she can lie beside him on the death platform."

"It always seems to be the women who get the worst end of things," Betty said, thinking back to the women she'd met who were kept as virtual hostages in their homes in Africa. "These people need to hear about the gospel message and the freedom it can bring them."

They trudged on, listening for any sign of the war party, but they heard none. Eventually, after hiking along a riverbank for three hours, Dugulugu raised his hand for them to stop. It was time for another conference with Leona. Once they were finished talking, five of the guides set off along the trail at a faster pace. Leona announced that they were going on ahead to let the people at Hitadipa know that the rest of the group would soon be there.

Betty was astonished at how quickly the men disappeared. She realized they had probably been walking at a slow pace for most of the trek so that she and Leona would not feel too pushed. She had no doubt they could have covered the distance of the trek in half the time.

By the time shadows were lengthening over the jungle, Betty and Leona and the rest of the party climbed one last ridge. The mission station at Hitadipa lay below them. Betty could clearly see the white house Bill Cutts had built and the airstrip to the right of it.

"The guides must have made it," Betty said with a chuckle. "Look at all the people waiting on the runway."

They quickened their pace now that the end was in sight. As they walked down the last ridge, Betty heard the strains of hymns being sung New Guinea style. She had never heard a hymn sound so welcoming before. They were nearly there, and they were safe.

The guides waved at them from the far side of the final stream that needed to be crossed and then waded over to help the women. Finally, after three days of hard slogging over mountains and through dense jungle, they had arrived.

The Cuttses proudly showed Betty and Leona around their new house. They had very few belongings, and after the trek to get there, Betty could understand why. Still it was great to be in a house, drinking coffee and eating sweet potatoes the locals had supplied.

The next morning Betty awoke early. She was eager to see how good a job Bill and the native men had done on the airstrip. She walked from one end of it to the other and back again. Then she moved over two yards and repeated the procedure, looking for anything that might be sticking up or any soft spots in the ground. She found none. The airstrip was perfect, except for an outcrop of rocks at the very front edge of the runway. The rocks were too big to move, but there was plenty of room to avoid them as long as a pilot knew they were there.

By the time Betty got back to the house, Grace Cutts and Leona St. John had preparations for breakfast well under way. As they ate, Bill Cutts radioed George Boggs that Betty had inspected the airstrip and everything was fine. He also made George aware of the rocks on the front edge of the runway. George thanked Bill for the news and promised to fly in at eleven that morning if weather conditions stayed favorable.

By 10:30 A.M. a crowd of Moni people had gathered at the airstrip. They sang hymns back and forth to one another and took turns shouting out Bible verses they had memorized. On the dot of eleven, a faint humming sound that grew louder and louder could be heard. Soon a Cessna 180 was circling directly overhead, and the group on the ground went wild, cheering and dancing. Finally Bill Cutts yelled to the crowd in their language above the noise, pointing to the edge of the airstrip as he did so.

"He's telling them to sit down because the plane has invisible knives that could cut them to pieces,"

Grace Cutts told Betty. "That's the best way he could think of to describe the propeller."

After about two minutes, Bill's words had achieved the desired effect, and the group sat cross-legged at the edge of the airstrip. By now, George had circled the Cessna and had it lined up for a landing. Betty glanced up at the makeshift wind-sock Bill had constructed. A gentle breeze was blowing from the southeast, perfect for a landing on the new airstrip.

George touched the wheels of the Cessna down about twenty feet in front of the rocks and rolled the plane to a stop. Bill held his hands out for the people to stay seated until the propeller had stopped turn-ing. Then he smiled and motioned for them to stand. Betty watched as the crowd surged forward, each person eager to touch the "canoe from the sky," as they called the airplane, and to talk with the man who had been "carried in its belly."

It was a day of singing, dancing, feasting, and celebrating. It was a day Betty would never forget as she saw firsthand how much an MAF airplane meant not only to the missionaries but also to the local people. The plane was a lifeline for them, a way to get a doctor in to visit them or to fly to one of the coastal towns for treatment if they became very ill.

The celebrating went on into the evening. George told Betty he was having so much fun that he had decided to spend the night. The next morn-ing, he, Betty, and Leona flew out of Hitadipa. They dropped Leona back at Homejo before setting off for Nabire, where Betty picked up her Cessna 180. The two airplanes then flew back to Homejo, where they loaded up the rest of the Cuttses' household wares and supplies. They ferried these to Hitadipa. Betty became the second pilot to land on the new airstrip there.

The Cuttses were grateful to finally have their household belongings, which Betty and George helped carry to the new house. Now with a folding table and chairs in the living room, the house was looking like a real home. Finally Betty left Hitadipa and flew back to Sentani, where that night she enjoyed a long, relaxing bath. Her muscles still ached from the three-day trek, but she didn't regret making it one bit. She had never quite experienced anything like walking down the mountainside while the voices of Moni Christians singing hymns echoed through the lush vegetation. Nor would she ever forget the tears streaming down Grace Cutts's face as she thanked Betty for her help. It made her feel proud to have had the privilege of being a part of something like MAF from its start.

Wings to Serve

After eighteen months of flying in New Guinea, Betty returned home to the United States. Once again, Christians around the country wanted to hear about her flying experiences. She set off on a speaking tour, crisscrossing the country as she told people about her flying adventures, the help airplanes were to missionaries in the field, and the need for more Christians to become involved in missions. After the speaking tour, she returned to MAF headquarters in Fullerton, California, where she served as corporate secretary on the organization's board of directors.

One of the happiest duties in her new position was to meet with young pilots who wanted to serve with MAF. It excited Betty to think that something that had started out as a simple idea in the hearts and minds of four military personnel in the waning days of World War II had blossomed into such a large and successful organization, with pilots and airplanes serving missionaries in many regions of the world.

Betty's other joy back at the office in Fullerton was coordinating the monthly prayer letter, which had grown out of the small Tuesday night prayer meetings she had held at the Trotmans' home as she worked to establish MAF. Now MAF staff around the world sent in their prayer requests, and Betty would condense them into a prayer letter that was sent to thousands of supporters. Although she had no more overseas flying assignments, she did get to fly in the United States, mostly ferrying new MAF airplanes from the factory to New Orleans, where they were packed and shipped to overseas locations.

After several years working with MAF in California, Betty realized that her parents were becoming aged and frail, and needed someone around to look after them. She knew it was time for her to go home to Medina, as the Evergreen Point area where the family home stood was now called. Throughout the remainder of her life, Betty stayed linked to MAF, continuing to coordinate the prayer letter from her home and taking on short speaking tours. She also loved to visit Bellevue Christian School, the school her two older brothers had started, and talk to the students. The school had grown from nine students to over eight hundred.

In 1976 her father died, followed in 1981 by her mother.

In 1990, at the age of seventy, Betty began to notice some strange things about her own behavior. She would drive to the grocery store and forget where to turn off the freeway to get home, or she would begin to write down her phone number and forget the last four digits. She went to see her doctor, and the diagnosis was inescapable. Betty Greene had Alzheimer's disease. Alzheimer's slowly causes a person's memories to fade until in the end the person is unable to remember the names of family members or even his or her own name.

Betty battled to stay active and alert as long as she could. Her old and dear friend Dorothy Mount, who had been Grady Parrott's secretary for many years, moved into an apartment nearby so she could care for Betty. When Betty became more forgetful, women at the First Presbyterian Church of Bellevue made up a roster of helpers so that someone would be with her twenty-four hours a day. It was particularly painful for her family, especially her twin brother Bill, to watch Betty lose her memory. The woman who had navigated her way across the Sahara Desert, flown over the Andes Mountains, and piloted numerous military aircraft could no longer find her way in her own home.

In early April 1997, Betty Greene caught a bad cold. When she recovered, she was unable to eat. She lay contentedly in her bed, staring out at the broadleaf maple trees in bud, the sparkling cold water of Lake Washington, and the gently sloping banks where she and Bill had collected buckets of blackberries seventy years before.

One day the woman looking after Betty tiptoed into the room to see whether she was awake and found her propped up on a pillow, wide awake and smiling. "Do you know God?" Betty asked the woman in a clear voice.

"Yes, I do," the woman replied.

Betty's face lit up. "Isn't it wonderful!" she exclaimed.

Soon after that brief conversation, Betty fell into a coma, and on April 10, 1997, she died. Her funeral, held at First Presbyterian Church of Bellevue, was titled a "Celebration of the Life of Betty Greene." Although many people mourned her passing, there was also much to celebrate.

Today Betty Greene's dream to use airplanes to serve missionaries lives on. Indeed the organization she helped found is alive and flourishing. Missionary Aviation Fellowship-United States now operates eighty-four aircraft from forty-seven bases located in nineteen countries. It is the world's largest fleet of private aircraft. Every four minutes, seven days a week, three hundred sixty-five days a year, a MAF-US airplane takes off or lands somewhere in the world. Each year these aircraft fly nearly five million miles, landing at some three thousand different airstrips while serving over five hundred Christian and humanitarian organizations. As well, MAF operates an extensive global communications network, from HF and VHF radio to satellite phones and an email system.

The strength and vibrancy of the organization today bears testimony to the farsightedness of the dream Betty and the other founders of MAF had back in 1945. These people desired to use wings to serve the cause of Christ. That is what they did, and Betty Greene played an important role in making it happen.

Buss, Dietrich G., and Glasser, Arthur F. *Giving Wings to the Gospel: The Remarkable Story of Missionary Aviation Fellowship.* Baker Books, 1995.

Carl, Ann B. *A Wasp Among Eagles: A Woman Military Test Pilot in World War II.* Smithsonian Institution Press, 1999.

Greene, Betty, with Dietrich G. Buss. *Flying High: The Story of Betty Greene* (unpublished manuscript).

Ringenberg, Margaret J. *Girls Can't Be Pilots: An Aerobiography.* Daedalus Press, 1998.

Janet and Geoff Benge are a husband and wife writing team with more than twenty years of writing experience. Janet is a former elementary school teacher. Geoff holds a degree in history. Originally from New Zealand, the Benges spent ten years serving with Youth With A Mission. They have two daughters, Laura and Shannon, and an adopted son, Lito. They make their home in the Orlando, Florida, area.

Also from Janet and Geoff Benge...

More adventure-filled biographies for ages 10 to 100!

Christian Heroes: Then & Now

Heroes of History

Available from YWAM Publishing
1-800-922-2143 / www.ywampublishing.com